THE
JADE KINGDOM

THE
JADE KINGDOM

THE JADE KINGDOM

Paul E. Desautels

 VAN NOSTRAND REINHOLD COMPANY
——————————————————————— New York

Library of Congress Catalog Card Number 86-5535

ISBN 0-442-21797-8

Printed in the United States of America

Designed by Karin Batten

Van Nostrand Reinhold Company Inc.
115 Fifth Avenue
New York, New York 10003

Van Nostrand Reinhold Company Limited
Molly Millars Lane
Wokingham, Berkshire RG11 2PY, England

Van Nostrand Reinhold
480 La Trobe Street
Melbourne, Victoria 3000, Australia

Macmillan of Canada
Division of Canada Publishing Corporation
164 Commander Boulevard
Agincourt, Ontario M1S 3C7, Canada

16 15 14 13 12 11 10 9 8 7 6 5 4 3 2 1

Library of Congress Cataloging-in-Publication Data

Desautels, Paul E.
  The jade kingdom.

  Bibliography: p.
  Includes index.
  1. Jade. 2. Jade art objects. I. Title.
QE394.J3D47 1986   553.8'7   86-5535
ISBN 0-442-21797-8

CONTENTS

PREFACE

Jade towers above all other hardstone carving materials—rose quartz, aventurine, agate, rock crystal, bloodstone, lapis lazuli, turquoise, and the rest—in both long-term popularity and sustained value. In spite of its intensive exploitation under widely diverse cultures, however, little authoritative work on the subject exists in the English language. When texts on jade do appear, they are usually little more than quick surveys of some of the more exotic carvings that have flowed, generation after generation, from the lapidary shops of China.

Of course, the history, lore, mineralogy, gemology, and art of jade can hardly be comprehended in the ideas ''green'' and ''China'': jade has been known for thousands of years, is widely found on the Earth's surface, and has been used extensively by several cultures. On the other hand, the Chinese have had the most to do with it, and the green varieties are consistently the most highly treasured. Eventually, Chinese jade carving became almost a pure art form, using many designs and symbols whose meanings are lost in the distant past or have become distorted in meaning through time. Little wonder, given this profusion of carvings—ancient and modern, primitive and sophisticated, religious and profane, symbolic and utilitarian, meaningful and meaningless—that study of (and writing about) jade has generally been the concern of artists, art historians, anthropologists, and archeologists.

The systematic study of jade is relatively new, and all sorts of impediments have slowed its development. Art historians and archeologists have always had great difficulty in identifying and dating jade objects that, through unscientific collection methods, have been divorced from the facts of their origins. Written records, when they exist, are often misleading. It is truly amazing that students have managed to sketch out a sequence of periods and styles spanning thousands of years, despite the haziness of many of the details of time and interpretation. Dozens of questions—such as when (within a century or two) diamond cutting tools were introduced into China, or where the high-quality jade found in ancient pre-Columbian sites was mined—may never be answered. An increasing effort has been made, however, to pull together evidence from various branches of science and bring it to bear on the more important questions. At least such erroneous inferences as the possibility of early commerce between China and Middle America have now been laid to rest. Speculation as to the Asiatic origin of European jade artifacts has died with the discovery of jade deposits in Europe itself. Slowly but surely, records of the ancient jade carvings of several cultures are being improved as the raw data yield to continuing scientific study and become more coherent.

Complicating the entire procedure has been one fundamental puzzle: exactly what is jade? First of all, the word *jade* is a gemological term, not a scientific one. Mineralogical science has only recently turned its attention to the chemical and physical nature of jade, in comparison to the length of time jade has been in use. All jade-using cultures have known it as a stone that could be cut and carved, was extremely durable, could hold an edge despite rough use, and might also be beautiful. At various times, one or more of these characteristics was considered sufficient to justify classifying a stone as jade. Not until the work of Alexis Damour in the 1860s was a successful attempt made to identify precisely the chemical nature of nephrite and jadeite, the two major kinds of jade. Since Damour's time, accumulated analyses, together with field samplings of new and old deposits and samplings of artifacts of known origin, have refined Damour's definitions. Unfortunately, this has been done at the cost of complicating our understanding almost to the point of impracticality. Recent discovery of the chromium analogue of jadeite—called ureyite—and the developing appreciation of jades as rock mixtures rather than as pure mineral entities have tended to heighten public confusion about what jade is.

Whatever the state of current knowledge of jade, the facts are difficult to locate because they are badly scattered in obscure publications, and the work of assembling them into a cohesive story is tedious. This book attempts to rectify this dispersion of information by bringing together quantities of pertinent information about the nature of jade, its occurrences worldwide, the major cultures that have made use of it, how they have made use of it, and the technologies they have developed to master it.

THE JADE KINGDOM

ONE

TRUE JADE

The Ancient Understanding

No matter how much this or any other book discusses it, jade is destined to remain a stone of legend and mystery. It has steeped in the life and lore of great civilizations for so many centuries that we can never know all of the virtues, qualities, and powers that have been attributed to it.

In thinking about jade, for example, we are unlikely to associate jade with music; and yet the Chinese long considered jade slabs, cut into a series of chimes, as the ideal source of a distinctively pure and sweet sound, when struck sharply in the appropriate sequence. Noted gemologist George Kunz states that, when things were not going well, Confucius would soothe his nerves by playing the "musical stone." Obviously, as its story has unfolded, the word *jade* has evoked many different images for many millions of people.

In the Western world, we do not look on jade as having any metaphysical meaning. The persistent Chinese belief that jade is the essence of the virtues of charity, justice, modesty, wisdom, loyalty, and honesty has not been passed on to us. And yet, for reasons that seem to transcend its market value, Westerners have become increasingly fond of the stone. A constant procession of carved jades passes each year through the great auction sales rooms of Sotheby, Christie, and others, bringing prices that attest to this growing interest.

The Present Understanding

The celebrated name *jade* has been applied, at times, to a multitude of green and near-green (and for that matter, other-colored), translucent, tough stones that can be cut and carved into ornamental objects. Throughout its more than 4,000-year history, jade has borne a confusion of names, descriptions, and legends, applied by many generations of mankind. For most of this time, considerable uncertainty has existed as to just what kinds of stones are entitled to the noble name. It is true that modern mineralogical science supplies us with fairly precise measurements of the physics and chemistry of materials we now call jade, but problems persist. After millenia of confusion, no universal agreement has yet been reached about which materials were included in the category of jade in the past, which are to be considered jade now, and how these definitions are to be established.

Most texts and references simply announce that jade comprises two mineral species, jadeite and nephrite (tremolite-actinolite). If so, many prized and ancient "jade" objects in the world must be excluded because they are neither jadeite nor nephrite. In addition, many "jade" objects have proved to be mixtures of jadeite or nephrite (in highly variable proportions) and one or more of the other minerals with which they normally occur in nature. Although it seems logical, rational, and sci-

1

entific that workable definitions can be established —indeed, the laws of modern commerce and trade require it—the nonscientific, artistic, and gemological definitions will probably always remain somewhat loose. Definition, even today, sometimes seems more a matter of tradition, history, aesthetics, and art than of science.

The Chinese evidently nurtured the confusion about jade from the very beginning. In the most ancient Chinese writings where the word *yu* appears, it has the same meaning as *jade* and is often used loosely in much the same way as the latter term is used today. The term *yu* evidently included nephrite, jadeite, bowenite, and sometimes ordinary serpentine, agalmatolite (or soapstone), and even marble. In fact, it likely included more mineral species in early Chinese times than it has at any time since. Part of the early confusion of species came from the ancient practice of classifying the kinds of *yu* by color, origin, and other characteristics, rather than by our present-day system of chemical differentiation.

Berthold Laufer, American jade authority of half a century ago, reported that Li Shih-chen, a great sixteenth-century Chinese naturalist, recognized fourteen varieties of jade based on color and origin. For example, the name *fei-ts'ui* (meaning kingfisher) was given to a beautiful green nephrite from Turkestan. Later this name was revived and applied to the emerald-green stone from Burma; the original Turkestan *yu* thereupon became *chen yu*, or "true" jade. By right of priority, then, nephrite—the original Turkestan type of stone—should carry the name *jade*, and the new, similar-looking but different material introduced from Burma (and now called jadeite) should not.

Fate and the evolution of language were to rule otherwise. Present-day, knowledgeable Chinese (and Westerners, too) now acknowledge both nephrite and jadeite as true jade. So it seems that, after centuries of people's not knowing or not caring, a decided drift has taken place toward excluding all other species, even bowenite and common serpentine, in favor of nephrite and jadeite as sole inheritors of the name *yu* or *jade*. This still does not resolve the problem that jadeite and nephrite occur frequently and in highly variable mixtures with other minerals and that the internal compositions themselves of these two minerals may also vary somewhat without totally losing their mineralogical identities.

Origins of the Name

The origins and conception of the word *yu* are lost in antiquity. The name *jade*, however, can be traced to its beginnings with considerable certainty. It evidently first appeared in print in England in 1727, in *Chambers Encyclopedia*. Despite such late publication, much evidence indicates that the material was known in Europe long before it had been assigned its new English name.

When Marco Polo traveled in the Orient in the late 1200s and visited Turkestan, he recognized the stone—actually nephrite—being recovered from streambed gravels. He referred to it as "jasper," but he was merely using the name he knew best for such stones. *Jasper* remained the name commonly used for jade in Europe until 300 years later, when Central American jade was brought home by the Spanish Conquistadors. The Portuguese may, however, have already been using the term *piedra de mijada* (meaning urinary stone, from its use as a treatment for urinary problems) for jade imported from China before the Spaniards entered the picture.

By the middle of the sixteenth century, Portuguese trade with China had so prospered that the Chinese permitted the Portuguese to purchase the peninsula at the mouth of the Canton River to use as a trade center. Here the city of Macao was established in 1557. At the time, there certainly existed an illicit trade in *yu*, which the Chinese considered very precious for reasons that included its supposed healing abilities. In particular, by mere surface application, it was thought to cure or prevent kidney and urinary diseases. The Spanish might well have borrowed the name and reputation of the stone from the Portuguese during this period of bustling trade and commerce. Nonetheless, there seems to be no identifiable reference to jade in the mineralogical or pharmacological writings of Europe before the discovery of jade in Central America.

When fifteenth-century Spanish explorers arrived in the New World, their attention was attracted to the green *chalchihuitl* objects so highly prized by the native people. Expecting tribute in gold and (later) emeralds, the conquistadors were surprised instead to be offered this green kind of "jasper."

In an official report on *The Discoverie of Guiana* in 1596, Sir Walter Raleigh makes note of "spleen stone" and "kidney stone," as this jade was then known because of its use in treating kidney diseases.

By Raleigh's time, the Spaniards were already familiarly calling it *piedra de hijada* (loin stone) or *piedra de los riñones* (kidney stone). By this time, too, the stones and stories of their curative powers had been introduced into Europe. Interestingly, no evidence suggests that the Aztecs themselves used the stone for curative purposes; that idea evidently came from elsewhere.

In the Latin used in all learned texts of that period, the stone's name became *lapis nephriticus* (kidney stone). In the late 1500s, by which time Nicolas Monardes, a Spanish physician, and others were writing of the *piedra de hijada*, the supply from Mexico had all but disappeared. Nearly a century after the conquest, the entire known American supply had been almost exhausted. Existing carvings had been plundered, and the natives had lost personal and cultural interest in the stone. Then, carvings made from a similar-looking stone began to appear in some quantity in Europe from the Orient, and these were promptly dubbed *piedra de ijada* or *lapis nephriticus*.

Belatedly it would be learned that this stone was not at all the same as the American kidney stone; some time afterward, it acquired the name *nephrite* by which it is known now. Sir Hans Sloane, a famous English natural historian, wrote about this same *piedra de ijada* in the early 1700s, but he still called it "green jasper." *Piedra de ijada* was absorbed into French as *pierre de l'ejade*, and somehow the French word *l'ejade* became *le jade*—evidently through a simple error in spelling. *Le jade* followed the path of many French words into English and became *jade*.

Earliest Jade Analysis

The mystery of the true mineral nature of jade was unraveled by Alexis Damour, a French chemist and mineralogist, who in 1863 published the results of his investigations showing that true jade was really two superficially similar mineral species. In his work, Damour used several jade carvings that had been taken by the English and French armies from the Imperial Summer Palace near Peking. The Palace was looted and destroyed in 1860 as a reaction to the treatment of European envoys in China during the 1859 T'ai P'ing Rebellion. Count Klaczkowski, who was in Peking at the time, brought back to Paris some jade objects of an unusually fine green color that intrigued Damour. Finally he unlocked their secret: they had a different chemical composition from the usual Chinese jades.

To one jade, the early Chinese type, Damour assigned the already existing name *nephrite*, which had been given to jade of the Chinese type in 1789 by A. G. Werner, a noted German mineralogist; it is a mineral species belonging to a family that present-day mineralogists call amphiboles. The other new type, comprising the *piedra de hijada* of the Spaniards and Count Klaczkowski's green stones, Damour gave the new name *jadeite*; it is a mineral species belonging to a family we now call pyroxenes.

Nephrite

Chemically, nephrite is a calcium-magnesium-iron silicate and is part of the species series known to mineralogists as tremolite-actinolite. Samples of members of this amphibole series theoretically may be found with compositions ranging from pure calcium-magnesium silicate (called tremolite) to a calcium-magnesium-iron silicate called actinolite. Pure tremolite is almost white, but in the series different samples may contain variable amounts of iron and thus—even in the absence of coloring introduced by mineral impurities—may range from pale green to deep green in color. It takes very little iron to give tremolite a greenish tint, and the color deepens considerably as the amount of iron increases.

Not all samples of tremolite-actinolite, however, can correctly be called nephrite. A qualifying specimen must be formed by nature in such a way that the microscopically fine fibrous crystals of which it is composed are tightly matted, tufted, and locked together, producing a compact, extremely tough, even-textured mass that has acceptable carving, durability, and surface luster characteristics. Because of these matted fibrous crystals, nephrite is tough enough to resist experimental pressures of over 90,000 pounds per square inch before crumbling.

Owing to variable amounts of iron and to certain impurities often present, nephrite may be white, yellow, green, red, brown, gray, black, or (rarely) blue. As we might expect, the Chinese had many names for the colors of nephrite. Eight names used commonly in the past for some of the more desirable colors are *sen*, a clear translucent white; *cha*, a highly prized opaque white; *pi*, an indigo blue; *pih*, a moss green; *kau*, a yellow; *chiung*, a cinnabar red; *men*, a blood red; and *haieh*, a lacquer black. There may well have been many more such names, con-

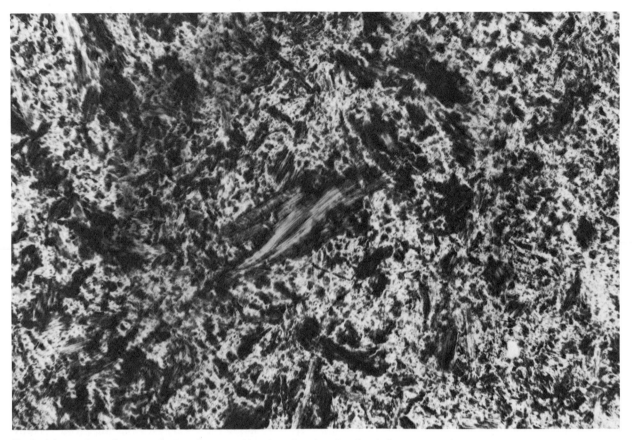

Rock thin section, photographed under magnification, showing details of the texture of nephrite from the Sweetwater River area of Wyoming.

sidering the old Chinese quotation: "There are 100 colors of white jade." Boulders of nephrite or carved objects that have been exposed to the effects of weathering for long periods of time develop a brownish alteration skin, sometimes of considerable thickness.

Nephrite jade is not extremely hard, measuring only 6½ on a hardness scale of ten, and is actually softer than rock crystal or amethyst. Its toughness, however, more than makes up for the difference and permits the material to be cut into delicate yet damage-resistant carvings. At the same time, its hardness of 6½ suffices to prevent most accidental surface scratching and abrasion damage that might occur through careless handling. The density of nephrite is about three times that of water (its specific gravity ranges from 2.90 to 3.01).

Jadeite

Jadeite, the other jade described by Damour, is a sodium-iron-aluminum silicate and is a member of the pyroxene group of minerals. Its color may vary, as does nephrite's, to include shades of bright emerald green due to the presence of very small amounts of chromium in place of iron. Occasionally, the chromium concentration is sufficiently high (with accompanying intensification of the green color) to change the nature of the stone itself to a bright green, sodium-chromium silicate species of the pyroxene group. This compound, named ureyite in honor of the famed chemist Harold Urey, was identified for the first time as an accessory mineral in certain meteorites recovered at Coahuila and Toluca in Mexico, and in the Hex River Mountains of South Africa. It turned out to be very nearly the same chemically as an earlier-described mineral species called cosmochlor, which had been found in materials of Earth origin in 1968. Since that time, ureyite itself has been found in several jadeite deposits on Earth.

Pink, mauve, blue, bluish gray, gray, white, red, orange, yellow, and black are other possible colors for jadeite. Many shades of green and of mottled green and white have also been found. Some con-

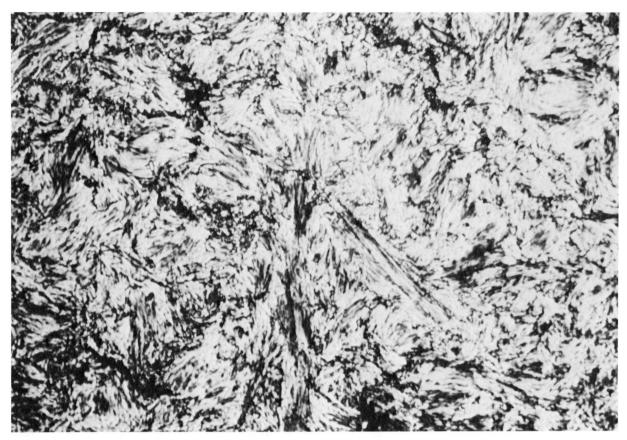

Rock thin section, photographed under magnification, showing details of the texture of nephrite from the Arahura River, Westland, New Zealand.

noisseurs believe that jadeite is superior to nephrite in the range and purity of its colors. Much of the jadeite found in Burma is white with spots and blotches that approach rich emerald green and possess high translucency. This is the well-known ''imperial jade,'' or *fei-ts'yu* of the Chinese.

Burmese jade merchants, of course, have developed their own color classifications for native jadeite: *mya yay* or *yay kyauk* for translucent grass green; *shwelu* for light green with bright green markings; *lat yay* for clouded material; *maw sit sit* for very dark green; *konpi* for red or brownish; *kyauk atha* for translucent white; *pan tha* for translucent white with opaque patches; and *kyauk ame* for green so dark that it appears black.

Whereas nephrite's texture is fibrous and matted, the small individual crystals of jadeite are more granular and give the material strength by their close interlocking. Recent studies show that much of the toughness of jadeite is due to the interruption of what would be the easy cleavage of each grain as it reaches the grain boundaries, leaving the remainder of the grainy mass intact. Because of its granular texture, jadeite is not as tough as nephrite, but both are tough enough to be more difficult to cut and carve than some harder and more precious stones. Jadeite is slightly harder (7 on a scale of 10) and denser (with a specific gravity of 3.30 to 3.36) than nephrite. The difference in specific gravity for the two species has proved to be the best simple basis for distinguishing them.

Jadeite Varieties

Certain less-well-known varieties of jadeite are worth mentioning because of their beauty and because they have been used in important carvings. Chloromelanite is dark green or blackish; part of it may actually be ureyite, which in some cases is quite dark. Chloromelanite is usually not a very pure jadeite, and some of it may even have a composition intermediate between jadeite and another dark-colored, sodium-iron silicate species called acmite. Mesoamerican jades, in particular, may contain

Rock thin section, photographed under magnification, showing details of the texture of jadeite from Clear Creek, California.

complex mixtures of jadeite, acmite, and a calcium-magnesium silicate called diopside. Dr. George Harlow, mineralogist and jade authority at the American Museum of Natural History, has even studied a jadeite sample in which the boundaries between grains are rich in glaucophane, a dark colored amphibole mineral that gives the entire mass an intense, dark color. Another of his samples, from Guatemala, is almost jet black.

The complex composition of most known jadeite samples again serves to emphasize that jades are not pure mineral species. For this reason, attempts at precise definition seem unlikely to prove successful, making the nonscientific definitions of ancient stonecutters and connoisseurs seem much more practical. The Mayans were satisfied to call a stone jade if it looked like it, carved like it, and had the appropriate durability.

Much of the jadeite found in Middle America is diopside-jadeite, which is intermediate between the two species even though it may look like pure jadeite. Frequently, jadeite samples consist of fine-to-coarse mixtures of these and other minerals such as zoisite and (even more commonly) albite—a distantly related white silicate mineral that belongs to a group of minerals known as plagioclase feldspars. Some Mesoamerican jade artifacts have proved to be white to greenish albite with little or no jadeite present. Still another variety of jadeite, called szechenyite, which is said to be from Burma, has been shown to be a variable mixture of ureyite, jadeite, and eckermanite (another amphibole mineral).

Other Jades

Several terms in popular usage describe still other kinds of jade; these names give the impression of

Rock thin section, photographed under magnification, showing details of the texture of chloromelanite from the Susa area of Italy.

identifying different species mixtures, but in fact they do not. "Mutton fat" jade, for example, is really just nephrite that contains very little iron and therefore has a pale gray-green color approaching white. When polished, it resembles solidified lard, thereby living up to its name.

"Chicken bone" jade has an opaque, chalky appearance, and its surfaces are usually covered with tiny cracks. In experiments conducted at the Freer Gallery in Washington, D.C., samples of both nephrite and jadeite were subjected to temperatures up to 1,025° C. Under such treatment, the nephrites altered to material of an opaque, chalky beige color, assuming the appearance of chicken bone jade without destroying or distorting any carved surface features. Subsequent X-ray diffraction identification showed that the nephrite had been chemically altered to diopside by the intense heat treatment, and so was no longer true jade. The jadeite samples that were heated the same way fused into a glassy sub-

stance, deforming any carved surfaces. Realization of the true nature of chicken bone jade has brought into circulation the much less picturesque name of *burnt jade*.

"Buried" jade refers to very ancient carved pieces that have become chemically altered after centuries of burial in tombs. Such jade is relatively fragile and has taken on a brown to blackish-brown color due to absorption of other tomb substances with which it has been brought into contact by percolating ground water solutions.

Semijade is a handy term for describing samples in which nature's process for converting amphibole- and pyroxene-forming rocks into jade was interrupted before completion. The Sir Charles Hardinge jade collection at the Gulbenkian Museum in Durham, England, includes a Chinese carving in a form called *ts'ung*. Sir Charles has described it as weighing 12 pounds, 9 ounces and as being made from actinolite-tremolite; it is not considered to be jade,

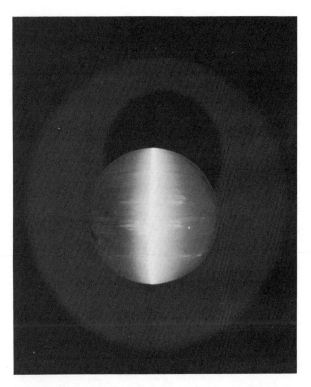

Cabochon gem cut from cat's-eye nephrite. Traces of the tiny fibrous bands that cause the light-band reflection are visible.

however, because the fibers lack the compactness of nephrite jade. Another carving in the collection is described as "tremolite jade," or "seminephrite," for the same reason. Undoubtedly, many of the world's fine nephrite carvings would more accurately be called seminephrite in recognition of the fact that, despite having the correct chemical composition, they were not completely transformed by nature into the finely fibrous, compactly matted material properly known as nephrite.

In recent years, an almost asbestoslike material has been found—of nephrite composition but with all the fibrous crystals parallel to each other. When properly cut in rounded cabochon style, the material produces an excellent cat's-eye effect attributable to reflections from the fibers. Although it has been called cat's-eye nephrite, some authorities say that the name is inappropriate because the material lacks the random intermatting of fibers present in true nephrite. This will remain a subject of controversy until general agreement is reached on how matted or felted the fibers of any mass must be before the material qualifies as jade.

POINT SOURCE OF LIGHT

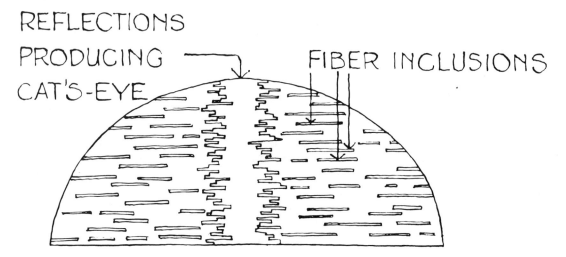

REFLECTIONS PRODUCING CAT'S-EYE

FIBER INCLUSIONS

The myriad light-band reflections are caused by fiber inclusions in the jade.

TWO

FALSE JADE

Innocently mistaking some other mineral substance for jade is always possible; then, too, individuals sometimes purposely use less valuable materials to deceive unwary buyers. Jade has many plausible imitations and substitutes, almost all of which are green or near green (since stone of this color is more easily mistaken or accepted as a plausible replacement for true jade). Some of the substitutes match the real thing so closely that even jade experts must be very careful when identifying samples and almost always rely on complicated tests when any doubt exists.

The Best Substitutes

The most common jade substitutes are serpentines, a group of magnesium-iron silicate minerals that occur in the same kinds of deposits as true jade and assume attractive, even beautiful, shades of blackish to emerald to yellowish green. Serpentine carves easily and well; some samples are so translucent as to approach transparency. Normally, serpentine can be distinguished quickly from either of the true jades because it is so soft—rarely reaching a hardness of over 4, as compared with hardnesses of 6 to 7 for jade. In addition, it usually has a specific gravity of just under 2.6, as compared with 2.9 to 3.4 for the jades. One variety of serpentine, however, called bowenite or Soochow jade, is much harder than most serpentines because of the way it was formed; it may have a specific gravity of slightly over 2.6 and a hardness of about 5½, figures close to the lower limit

figures for nephrite (which it closely resembles). At times bowenite is troublesome to distinguish from nephrite, but to the practiced eye its luster on polished surfaces differs considerably; and this, when combined with hardness and specific gravity determinations, unmistakably identifies it.

Idocrase (more correctly known as vesuvianite), a calcium-magnesium-aluminum silicate mineral, is seldom confused with jade except in its very compact greenish variety, called californite, which may even have colorless or white streaks in it that increase its resemblance to jade. Occurring in several California counties and elsewhere around the Earth, idocrase is not easy to distinguish by ordinary tests. A relatively new source of californite in California has produced a quantity of material ranging in color from a very pale, opaque, creamy green to various shades of lime green to a deep, jadelike lime-olive green. Californite's hardness of 6½ overlaps the jades and its specific gravity of 3.3 to 3.5 puts it near their top densities. More sophisticated testing is essential to exclude this species, although experts can often detect it by subtle color and luster differences.

Even one member of the garnet family of minerals may masquerade as jade. It is a greenish to rose variety called hydrogrossular and is a calcium-aluminum silicate. This compact, even-textured mineral is found at Buffelsfontein and Turffontein farms, 40 miles west of Pretoria in the Transvaal of South Africa, which accounts for the name under which it is marketed *(Transvaal jade)*. Aside from the fact that it does not look much like jade (even to the semitrained eye), it can be detected by simple tests. Its specific gravity varies from 3.42 to 3.55, putting it outside the jade range, although its hardness (just over 7) is close enough to pose problems if this test alone is used.

Other Mineral Substitutes

Several varieties of quartz and quartz-bearing rocks vaguely resemble jade. Even if visual differences were insufficient to separate the quartz group from jades, the very low specific gravity (2.6) of quartz would be enough. One possible interloper from this group is aventurine quartz, which would be colorless but for its myriad tiny flakes of green chrome mica, called fuchsite, which give it an overall green color as well as an internally sparkling effect. Jasper and carnelian, the brown and red fine-grained varieties of quartz, resemble certain of the nongreen jades, but again their low specific gravity and different surface luster give them away. This is also true of moss agate and certain other agates that consist of fine-grained quartzes with internal inclusions and color mottlings similar to those of some jades.

The closest look-alike among the quartzes is chrysoprase, a fine-grained quartz that, thanks to the presence of a small amount of nickel, occurs in beautiful shades ranging from apple green to dull yellow-green. Most chrysoprase greens are totally unlike jade green. It cuts and carves well and is altogether a pleasing stone, but because of its relative unavailability it has generally been limited to use in small objects such as beads, cabochons, and small carvings. In recent years, however, a considerable quantity of chrysoprase of the highest quality from a new discovery in Australia has permitted its use for larger carvings. Beads and cabochons of this newer material at times look very much like the finest jadeite and may even be mistaken for imperial jade.

A number of other mineral species have been pressed into service as jadelike gem materials, but more for their own beauty than as passable substitutes for jade. They make attractive (though usually fragile) objects of art, and they are sometimes mistaken for jade. Carving forms and techniques designed for a tough material like jade cannot possibly work with materials that do not possess the same properties; as a result, such materials typically lack the elegant and delicate features we have come to expect in jade carvings.

Fluorite—a calcium fluoride—for example, occurs in attractive transparent to translucent masses suitable in quality and size for carving. Its hardness number is so low (4), however, and it tends to cleave so easily that carving and polishing an intricate design are almost impossible. Still, because it is soft, fluorite cuts easily, and it is beautiful in its own right—although it looks nothing like jade.

Smithsonite, a blue-green to green (and sometimes even yellow) zinc carbonate, is another soft (5 in hardness), aesthetically pleasing mineral used for carving. It, too, fails to resemble jade at all closely. Additional examples of the same type include prehnite, a yellow-green calcium-aluminum silicate; amazonite, a potassium-aluminum silicate and a member of the feldspar family; and pinite, a massive and compact form of muscovite mica.

A very rare chromium-bearing variety of the mineral epidote, a calcium-aluminum-iron silicate, is deep green in color. It is found in Tawmaw in the Kachin hills of Upper Burma, bears the common name *tawmawite,* and has been used to simulate jade. Although all tawmawite has been considered an epidote variety for many years, recent investigations indicate that at least some of it is really ureyite.

In short, almost every known greenish mineral that lends itself to carving has been used and confused at one time or another with jade.

Rock Substitutes

Rocks, which can be described as rather variable mixtures of several minerals, have added their share to the confusion. The jades are rocks, of course, but rocks of other compositions should be mentioned as potential substitutes. For example, smaragdite, a metamorphic rock, is an emerald green foliated variety of amphibole. When sufficiently even-textured and compact in form, it is almost indistinguishable from jadeite; and in fact, distinguishing between the two by simple means may not be possible.

Several other rocks, some of them rather strange mixtures, also make reasonably good jade substitutes. Astridite, for example, is the trade name of a dark green rock found in New Guinea that reportedly is an intergrowth of jadeite, picotite, quartz, opal, and limonite.

Agalmatolite is a favorite Chinese carving stone of mixed composition and nondescript appearance. It often occurs as a natural alteration product of the mineral cordierite, and sometimes it is found in very large rock deposits and called steatite, or soapstone. It may be gray, greenish, brownish, yellowish, black, or an odd blend of two or more of these hues. Soft enough to be scratched by a fingernail, and characterized by a dull, waxy luster, it is not very attractive and not at all durable. For many years, it has served as the base material for carvings of grotesque images and objects that are frequently sold to the uninformed and unobservant as jade. Older oriental carvings of agalmatolite have become collectors' items because of their age, but certainly not because of their beauty or intrinsic value.

Dyed Jade and Dyed Quartzite

All the materials discussed so far are natural materials that people have not tampered with. Predictably, however, some materials—both jade and nonjade—owe their precise appearance to ancient or modern technology. The technique of dyeing stones, for example, has been practiced continuously for centuries. With the advent of all sorts of new chemical dyes, enhancing or approximating the color of jade is easier than ever. Since white or off-white jadeite is much more common than good green material, certain individuals have taken to dyeing the commoner stuff a fine imperial green, or some other desirable hue.

Depending on the dye and the care with which it has been applied, the results may be quite successful. The dye tends to concentrate in cracks and fissures, along grain boundaries, and in other openings, however, which allows it to be distinguished under magnification from true green jade (in which the color is distributed without regard to such boundaries). Dyed green jades are also susceptible to gradual fading, especially if exposed to heat, strong light, or other conditions that might destroy the dye. Highly prized mauve jadeite is also imitated by dyeing; in this case the pigment seems relatively stable, but the dyed color is usually made too

intense and automatically draws attention to the possibility of forgery. Again, dyeing can be rather easily detected by the telltale accumulation of dye along fissures, cracks, and grain boundaries or by mild heat treatment, which causes the dye to blacken or fade appreciably.

Another favorite stone for artificial coloration is a rock called quartzite. This rock is composed of small, granular, interlocking masses of quartz that have irregular boundaries with each other; it is much like jadeite in texture. The quartz grains themselves are impervious to the dye, but pigmentation spreads readily along the grain boundaries, giving a finished carving the appearance of remarkably good green jadeite.

Other Jade Forgeries

The ingenuity of jade forgers is hardly limited to dyeing. A favorite trick (though one declining in popularity now) is to prepare a ring or brooch stone with a white jade top and a separate white jade bottom and then cement these together with green cement or fill the hollow cavity between them with green dye before fastening the halves together. As long as the joining of the two parts is hidden in the jewelry mounting, the unsuspecting owner may have no inkling of the cheat. And since the enclosed color fades less easily than an exterior dye would, the deception can last a long time.

The use of various types of plastic and glass to simulate jade is much more readily detectable. In fact, these materials are so easy to spot that only the very gullible purchaser will be taken in by them. Even the nonexpert can quickly learn to identify the tiny bubbles or mold marks visible in glass under slight magnification. Plastics have a density far below that of jade; they consequently feel very light when they are hefted. In addition, most plastics are very soft and can be scratched easily with a needle. Some highly realistic glass and plastic imitations, however, have had to be sent to the laboratories of the Gemological Institute of America before positive identification could be made.

THREE

JADE TESTING

Jade would be easier to collect and study if some simple method for identifying true jade could be found. Unfortunately, no easy way lies within the reach of all. Most of the folklore about jade identification is absolutely worthless. Differences in luster are very subtle, and while jade may be cool to the touch, so are many other mineral substances. Therefore, a certain basic knowledge of the facts about jade, experience with it, and some specific testing equipment are indispensable.

When experts check jade, they usually work with three convenient characteristics. If these fail, they turn to other more sophisticated tests that are practically infallible at identifying what the material in question happens to be. The first three required tests are for hardness, specific gravity, and refractive index. The usually diagnostic but sometimes confusing fourth test is X-ray diffraction identification.

Hardness

Hardness in mineral materials is a measure of their resistance to scratching and general wear. Over the years, an inexact but practical hardness testing scale called the Mohs Scale of Hardness (named after the Austrian mineralogist Friedrich Mohs, who proposed it in 1822) has been generally adopted. It consists of a ranking of ten readily available minerals in order of increasing resistance to scratching: 1 talc, 2 gypsum, 3 calcite, 4 fluorite, 5 apatite, 6 feldspar, 7 quartz, 8 topaz, 9 corundum,

10 diamond. Nephrite, with a hardness of 6½ on this scale, can thus be scratched by a piece of quartz (H.7) but not by feldspar (H.6). Jadeite, with a hardness of 7, can be scratched by a piece of topaz (H.8) but not by feldspar (H.6), and it may or may not be scratched by a piece of quartz (H.7).

Table 3-1. Location of Nephrite and Jadeite on the Mohs Scale of Hardness.

1. Talc
2. Gypsum
3. Calcite
4. Fluorite
5. Apatite
6. Feldspar
6.5 *Nephrite*
7. Quartz
7.0 *Jadeite*
8. Topaz
9. Corundum
10. Diamond

Metal tools appropriately tipped with hardness points are available for hardness testing. Nephrite and jadeite can usually (but not always) be distinguished from each other by trying to scratch them with the quartz point of a hardness tool rated at H.7. Nephrite will scratch but jadeite usually will not. Unfortunately, the hardnesses of 6½ and 7 for true jade are close enough to those for some forms of bowenite, californite, and so on, that the test cannot be used to exclude all nonjades. Even so, it may be helpful when combined with other tests.

Specific Gravity

The specific gravity of any solid substance is a function of its weight in comparison to the weight of an equal volume of water. For example, a 1-inch cube of silver weighs 10½ times as much as a 1-inch cube of water, so the specific gravity of silver is 10.5. The Greek mathematician Archimedes is given credit for discovering, in the third century B.C., a simple method for determining the specific gravity of any solid. He realized that an object weighs less when submerged in water than it does in air, and that the weight loss is equal to the weight of the water displaced by the object. In other words, the weight loss represents the weight of a volume of water equal to the volume of the object.

Table 3-2. Specific Gravities of Various Minerals.

	2.5 } Serpentine (Bowenite)			
	2.6 }			
	2.7			
	2.8			
Nephrite {	2.9			
	3.0			
	3.1			
	3.2			
	3.3			
Idocrase {	3.4 } Garnet	} Jadeite		
	3.5			
	3.6			
	3.7			
	3.8			

To determine the specific gravity of a jade sample, the investigator simply weighs the sample accurately in air and weighs it again while it is immersed in water. The jade's weight in water is then subtracted from its weight in air, giving the weight of the displaced (equal) volume of water. Finally, this weight is divided into the weight of the jade in air to find the multiplication factor by which it exceeds the weight of the water. This factor is the specific gravity. Naturally, the better the weighing scale and the greater the accuracy with which the work is done, the higher the quality of the results will be.

If several jade samples are to be checked over a period of time to distinguish nephrite from jadeite, the sink-float method for determining specific gravity is convenient. This involves preparing a saturated solution of methylene iodide, which has a density of about 3.3 but can be diluted with toluene to attain a density of 3.0. Other laboratory equipment or a sample of known density must be used to check the density of any solution to be used in this type of testing. The jade is checked by dropping a small fragment of it into the solution. If the sample is jadeite, it will sink in the 3.0-density fluid because jadeite's specific gravity is in the range from 3.3 to 3.6; if it is nephrite, it will float or sink very slowly because its specific gravity is in the range from 2.9 to 3.01. These testing methods, like those for hardness, are useful but not always definitive.

Refractive Index

A substance's refractive index is a measure of its ability to bend a beam of light. Transparent to translucent solids will cause a beam of light to bend as it strikes and then passes through a surface; the degree of bending that occurs depends on the kind of light and the nature of the solid. A small instrument called a gem refractometer has been devised to measure this effect when a flat polished face of a small fragment of stone is placed against the upper stage and viewed through an eyepiece. The refractive index can be read directly from a scale in the eyepiece.

For jades, the readings are not sharp because of the diffusing effect of the material's granular or fibrous texture. Jadeite gives a diffuse reading of about 1.66, while nephrite gives a reading of about 1.62 also diffuse. If a relatively distinct reading is obtained (assuming, too, that the jade piece or carving fits on the refractometer and that the composition of the piece is fairly uniform), it should distinguish the true jades from any of their common substitutes.

Since Chinese tomb jades and natural jade boulders, as mentioned earlier, have typically experienced a surface alteration that leaves them with a soft, less dense, opaque coating, the coating will be responsible for misleading results in those tests. If possible, only fresh material should be used in testing.

X-ray Diffraction

One of the best methods for identifying jades and their substitutes is X-ray powder diffraction. Unfortunately, the procedures require professional training in the techniques of X-ray diffraction, and this means of testing is not generally available except in mineralogical laboratories. The results obtained from X-ray powder diffraction are based on the chemistry and atomic structure of the substance itself and thus constitute a direct means of identification. X-ray diffraction can fail miserably, however, when applied to certain rock mixtures that contain small amounts of nephrite or jadeite and large amounts of other minerals. Fortunately, when these situations arise, the test results will indicate that the piece is not primarily jade and that a different kind of X-ray diffractometer—one usually used for rock analysis—should be employed.

X-ray powder diffraction patterns for jadeite, nephrite, and the jade substitutes serpentine and vesuvianite.

Other Test Instruments

Quick, easy, and reliable determinations about jade mixtures and other kinds of rock can be obtained through the use of a petrographic microscope. Using this expensive piece of equipment, a trained microscopist who is accustomed to working with jades can very rapidly differentiate among the varieties of jadeite, between jadeite and nephrite, and between jade and many jadelike minerals. Best of all, only a small piece of material (which can be removed from some inconspicuous place on the main mass) is needed. Of course, everything depends on having an operator who is trained and experienced in the techniques of optical crystallography—especially with jades.

The primary laboratory tool used today for the study of mixed rock compositions is the electron microprobe analyzer. This efficient but very expensive device is capable of producing precise chemical analyses of each rock grain or even of the filling material between grain boundaries. Alas, the volume and precision of the data produced often serve to make simplified, practical definitions for jade even more difficult.

FOUR

SOURCES OF JADE

The Metamorphic Environment

Published reports of discoveries of jade deposits—present-day and ancient—may cumulatively give the impression that jade is common almost everywhere in the Earth's crust. This is at once true and misleading. Enormous quantities, sufficient to leave traces of artifacts scattered almost everywhere, have been found. Unfortunately, the bulk of it is poor to mediocre in quality; only a relatively small portion is sufficiently translucent, well-colored, and fine-textured to qualify as prized carving material. Considering the enormous demand for it and the few places where it occurs in a high-quality form, jade is a very rare gem material.

Both nephrite and jadeite occur in nature in metamorphic rock—rock that, after having already formed in the Earth's crust, was subjected to further structural and compositional changes by additional heat, pressure, liquids, and gases. Between the temperatures and pressures of a molten environment deep below the crust and the watery grave of a sedimentary environment lies an enormous range of changing conditions. Existing rocks are constantly subjected to change by the environmental agents named above; they respond by metamorphosing into new kinds of rocks possessing new kinds of constituent minerals. The jades are good examples of minerals and rocks created by metamorphic activity.

Nephrite and Jadeite Environments

Nephrite is typically associated with gneisses, schists, serpentines, marblelike metamorphosed limestones, and other metamorphic rocks. It is commonly found at contact points between rocks of dissimilar character that have been strongly metamorphosed. At such sites, it may lie in elongated, lenslike masses, in sheets, or in nodules.

When a nephrite deposit is attacked by erosion, the nephrite itself, being so tough and durable, defies environmental wear and tear long after these have destroyed the other rocks surrounding it. Thus it persists in streambeds as smoothed and rounded pebbles or as boulders that may weigh many tons. Much of the world's nephrite—particularly in its classic Asiatic occurrences, but also in Alaska and New Zealand—is recovered as stream-tumbled and -smoothed lumps.

This accounts for the procedure used by prospectors in searching for nephrite deposits. The first step is to find traces of jade pebbles or boulders in or near a streambed. These traces can then be followed upstream until a point is reached at which the traces disappear. At that point, either to the left or right and up out of the streambed, the original in-place deposit may be found (if it has not been completely eroded away).

Jadeite deposits occur much as do nephrite deposits: in masses, lenses, stringers, and nodules enclosed in strongly metamorphosed serpentinous rocks. The major difference is that rocks associated with jadeite must be rich in sodium. The abundance of sodium accounts for the frequent occurrence of albite, a sodium feldspar, in the same deposits with jadeite. Because jadeite has a granular or crystalline texture, as compared to the fibrous texture of nephrite, it produces alluvial boulders with greater surface alteration and less polish than appear on stream boulders of nephrite.

Eastern Jadeite

Good jadeite is far rarer than good nephrite. Except for the famous deposits in Burma and Guatemala, the world's supply of jadeite—either as artifacts or in rough form—is and always has been virtually insignificant. Burma has been the only consistent source of new quantities of high-quality jadeite. Some of this imperial jade is of such high quality that it commands prices equivalent to those of good emerald in the gem market.

Jadeite mining activity in Burma is centered in the villages of Tawmaw and Hpakan in the far north of Burma, not far from the borders of Tibet and Yunnan in China. The primary or in situ deposits formed as layers in metamorphosed serpentine rocks in contact with granites. These lie in the Kachin Mountains near Mogaung and in the valley of the Uru River (a tributary of the Chindwin River). Important deposits of alluvial boulders exist in the Uru River valley, with the chief occurrences being near the villages of Pakham, Hweka, and Mamon.

At the Tawmaw mines in the hills north of the Uru River, in situ jade mining is typical and has not changed much over the centuries. Fires are built on the rock face and then quenched with water so that the temperature shock cracks the rock. Workers then split out cracked chunks of it by hand, using hammer and wedge. The process is laborious and often results in serious damage to the jade.

Most of the jade from these deposits is a very pale green or off-white color. Because the material dyes easily, strong temptation exists to treat large quantities of it—and this is commonly done. Some of the jadeites are strongly green and even contain ureyite in significant amounts. *Maw sit sit,* recently found at the site by the noted gemologist Dr. Gubelin, owes its deep color to its being primarily ureyite.

Scattered reports indicate the presence of jadeite in the Chinese province of Yunnan. This is to be expected because Yunnan lies near the producing areas of Burma and because the great drainage systems of the Salween and Mekong rivers, which originate in mountainous Tibet, lie close to the Chindwin River system, and travel through the length of Yunnan.

Western Jadeite

The only other known source of carving jadeite—which is in Guatemala—has been primarily an object of historical and archeological interest following the collapse of Mesoamerican cultures under the Spanish conquest; no significant amounts of jadeite from that source have been fed into world commerce since then.

In 1952, Robert Leslie of the Smithsonian Institution found an 11-inch, roughly spherical boulder of jadeite in a newly plowed field on the north bank of the Motagua River. It proved to be very similar to the large masses found later at Kaminaljuyu and at San Cristóbal Acasaguastlan. Leslie's specimen showed traces of work scars left by someone's having knocked former protrusions off the surface. Directly above Manzanal, north toward the mountains, an outcropping of what appeared to be jade-bearing rock was found in plain sight, covering approximately 400 square feet. Analyses of jadeites from the general area proved the material of this boulder to be the same as that used in the archeological jadeite objects recovered from Olmec, Mayan, and the Aztec sites. Thus at least one source mystery was solved.

Recent fieldwork by Dr. George Harlow confirmed the occurrences of jadeite on the north side of the Motagua River valley and particularly along the valley of the Palmilla River, a tributary to the Motagua. He also confirmed the existence of a very large jadeite area on the north side of the Motagua River, to the west of the Palmilla River and stretching to the Huijo River. Old, abandoned jade and obsidian sources have both been found on this site; work at the jadeite sources has resumed in the past decade, and some rough material has been utilized for carvings in the Mayan style, produced and marketed by local artisans. On the whole, however, the quantity and quality of available material have had little market impact.

Other Jadeite Occurrences

Scattered, insignificant occurrences of jadeite artifacts have been reported elsewhere. Actual minor deposits have also been found—such as the one in contacts between schists and serpentines at a number of points along Clear Creek in San Benito County, California. Years ago, Russian jadeite samples were described by Soviet geologist N. L. Dobretsov from the polar Ural Mountains and also from the Borus Mountains (part of the West Sayan Mountains). The Borus occurrence is directly to the west of the great Siberian deposits near Lake Baikal. In the past decade, the quantity of jadeite has encouraged commercial exploitation; quantities of the rough material, in blocks and slabs, are now easily obtainable from a number of gemstone dealers. Other than this, none of the other discoveries shows promise as a potential source for future supplies of jadeite.

Alaskan Nephrite

The great nephrite resource in the Americas lies in Western Canada and Alaska. Early explorers of the Alaskan coast, the Yukon River, and the country eastward to the Mackenzie River and south along the coast of British Columbia found that nephrite jade was in general use by local Indians and Eskimos. They and later European visitors acquired large numbers of jade artifacts. Explorers including James Cook, George Vancouver, and the Comte de La Pérouse were impressed by the natives' use of this tough green stone.

The Alaskan Eskimos, who dug most of their nephrite boulders from the bed of the Kobuk River, spoke of the existence of an entire mountain of green stone along the river. In 1883, U.S. Navy Lieutenant George M. Stoney penetrated the area and rediscovered Jade Mountain, some 30 miles due west of the town of Kobuk, thus certifying the truth of Eskimo legends. The entire mountain is green, mostly from serpentine fragments that litter its slopes; but it also contains enormous deposits of nephrite. Many outcrops and many alluvial sources have been found, and it is certain that others will be discovered upon further exploration.

Nephrite jade occurs here in a broad area about 40 miles long, north of and roughly parallel to the Kobuk River, throughout a series of low, rounded mountains called the Jade Hills, and also appears in the form of boulders in surrounding streams. For example, the Dahl Creek area, which begins at the confluence of Stockley and Dahl creeks and then trends northward toward the summit of Mount Asbestos and then easterly, has proved to be quite productive. All of the terrain is incredibly rough and inaccessible, with no roads and a short, weather-limited season for prospecting; moreover, in 1980, a vast area just west of the Jade Mountains (and including part of the range) was set aside as Kobuk Valley National Park. For these various reasons, the rate of mining and transportation of the rock is severely restricted, resulting in a limited rate of exploitation of an evidently enormous supply.

Alaskan nephrites occur in attractive shades of olive green, yellow-green, gray-green, and blackish green. Some excellent pale greenish gray cat's-eye nephrite has been found. Kobuk nephrite, as a whole, is not as fine in texture or as varied in color as nephrite from Wyoming. Nonetheless, raw material from this area has been exported to centers such as Hong Kong and Paris. Much of it goes to Germany for cutting and polishing and then on to New Zealand and elsewhere for retail sale.

British Columbian Nephrite

British Columbian nephrite resources are also very large, the bulk of the supply in the past having come from the gravels and boulders of an enormous area along the lower reaches of the Fraser River. The deposits seem almost inexhaustible, and each spring's flood exposes additional polished boulders. Along the river (as well as in the Columbia River basin), large numbers of artifacts dating back as far as 1500 B.C. show the local tribes' very early familiarity with British Columbian sources. The pre-Columbian spread of this jade to many parts of what are now southwest Canada and northwest United States show that a brisk trade in jade had developed over the centuries.

In situ sources of Fraser River–type nephrite include those of the Omineca area of central British Columbia and the Frances Lake jade field in the Yukon; additional sites are likely to be discovered in the future. In the north of the province, the deposits at Dease Lake, off the Alaskan Highway, are typical. Taking the city of Dease Lake as the center, jade occurs in an area of fifty miles radius. At Cassiar nearby, *chrysotile asbestos,* mined as veinlets in serpentine matrix, has revealed associated nephrite and the heretofore ignored jade (which had been thrown into waste dumps) is now being recovered.

Dease Lake or Cassiar District nephrite is highly variable in its cutting quality. In addition to problems of limited accessibility in difficult terrain that are typical of many Alaskan and British Columbian jade deposits, the boulders here are often so large—weighing many tons each—that they are impossible to move or transport. And because of their great toughness, they are very difficult to divide into manageable pieces. British Columbian jade is found in several shades of green, like that from Alaska, as well as in a form that is grayish white with green spots. Jadeite is unknown in this part of the world.

From its anchor in Alaska and British Columbia, a nephrite jade chain extends all the way through California to Central America and into Brazil; existing artifacts carry the range archeologically into Argentina. A single nephrite deposit is known at Babytinga near Amargoza, Bahia in Brazil, but pieces have been found elsewhere in the country, and jade celts are known from the lands of Amazon River natives. Even more remarkable, pebbles of nephrite have been found from the shores of Lake Huron in Ontario southward through the glacial areas of Illinois, Iowa, Ohio, and Indiana. Others appear in the streambeds of Oaxaca, Mexico. It is as if the entire western hemisphere were loosely strewn with pebbles of nephrite.

This vast spread is not as surprising as it seems because the metamorphic rocks in which jades are found in the western hemisphere are more or less continuous from north to south. These formed when the upthrust of the western chain of mountains produced metamorphism of sediments carrying the constituents required for nephrite. Thus jade may exist almost anywhere in the cordilleras of North, Central, and South America.

California Nephrite

In California, jade has been typically found in small amounts in Marin County on the east slope of Massa Hill, in Tulare County on Lewis Hill, and in Trinity County in the streambed of the Upper Trinity River. Several jade sites have been found in the southern extension of the mother–lode gold country. Beginning 2½ miles north-northeast of Bagby, the jade area runs for about 12 miles to a point roughly 2 miles north of Coulterville. Jade mines in the area bear such fanciful names as Ming, Yang, Green Dragon, Four Jacks, and Jade King. Jade is found there both in situ and as alluvial float, but quantities of both are limited and good-quality material is scarce.

One other area in California deserves special mention because it has been a Mecca for jade fancying rock hounds for many years. This nephrite deposit lies approximately 70 miles south of Monterey on the coast; it was first discovered in 1941 by Spencer N. Parmalee and then rediscovered in 1947. The jade occurs as large alluvial boulders on the seacoast and offshore at some depth. When the collecting rush began the site was named Jade Cove. In situ nephrite in the area is associated with serpentine and with mylonite, a hard metamorphic rock type composed mostly of albite, quartz, and tremolite. It has been described in detail in Special Report 10A (by Richard Crippen) of the California Division of Mines.

Unfortunately, Monterey jade contains micalike inclusions and partings, which cause it to split rather easily along approximately flat planes and to display a silvery sheen. On the whole, the jade tends to be poorly translucent and nondescript in color. In years past, it was found by collectors in sizes ranging from small pebbles to enormous boulders. A book has even been written by Don Wobber about the experiences he and his friends had in recovering a 9,000-pound, 8-foot-long boulder from 30 feet underwater. Collectors generally find the pickings to be best at Jade Beach, just north of the cove, or at Willow Creek, 1 mile to the south. A peculiar kind of nephrite—in masses with rounded grapelike surfaces, called locally botryoidal jade—has been recovered on Cape Saint Martin at the south end of Willow Creek.

Wyoming Nephrite

The finest nephrite in the western hemisphere comes from Wyoming. The discovery of jade in this state is credited to William L. Marion and Lloyd B. Curtis, both of Lander, in 1936. Sporadic reports in the early 1930s of fine apple-green jade from near Crook's Mountain, 50 miles southeast of Lander, had been made; nevertheless, the Marion-Curtis discovery started a "jade rush," and by the mid-1940s several local families were selling Lander jade. Soon

Delicate double-handled cup, carved by George Ashley of lustrous, jet-black Wyoming nephrite. Photo courtesy of the Smithsonian Institution, Washington, D.C.

it became clear that Lander was on the edge of what was at that time the most important jade area in the hemisphere.

As might be expected, the nephrite is associated with serpentine adjacent to schists and granites. It is found in an enormous belt measuring approximately 140 miles east to west, with a maximum width of 60 miles, and takes in portions of Sublette, Sweetwater, Fremont, Natrona, and Carbon counties. The Sweetwater River runs along its axis. Another large jade area lies just to the south, in the Saratoga Basin of Carbon County, flanked by the Sierra Madres and the Medicine Bow Mountains.

Although Wyoming jade is seldom free of black specks and other inclusions—including at times complete, clear quartz crystals—it compares very well with the best Asiatic nephrite. The jet-black and fine green Wyoming jades that can be polished to a mirror finish are very rare, but they rate among the best of their kind in the world. The area has also produced quality jades in near-white, gray, yellow, bluish green, brown, red, and even dark green with spots of red resembling bloodstone. Most of it is a darkish green often relieved with blotches and mottlings of light-colored tremolite, pink zoisite, or other inclusions.

Jade recovery continues in Wyoming, though the earlier (and more frantic) collecting days are gone now that the area has been swept bare of easily found surface material. Large, fine masses are still being gleaned from in situ and alluvial sources. Perhaps the largest mass preserved for public view is in the Field Museum of Natural History in Chicago; weighing 2,500 pounds, it was a gift of jade-lover James Kraft. Many museums, knowingly or not, have prized carvings of Wyoming jade that are touted to be Chinese. Wyoming nephrite justifiably holds a position of honor as the state gem.

Most descriptions of nephrite occurrences in North America give the impression that deposits are restricted to its western parts, and most are indeed located there. However, nephrite has also been reported from such places as Christianshaab in the Disko Bay area of southwest Greenland, where it is found with serpentine and massive soapstone, and farther south near Godthaab, where it appears as rounded greenish lumps in talc. Such widespread occurrences underscore the fact that much of the Earth's crust is covered with metamorphic rocks of a kind that can contain jade.

Asian Nephrite

On the other side of the world, nephrite is again more abundant than jadeite. Some of the largest deposits are in New Zealand and Russia, whose recovery efforts have been watched with interest because of their potential impact on the world's supply. In New Zealand, the modern cutting and carving industry is centered at the west-coast town of Hokitika on the South Island, although there are also North Island factories. The demand for rough jade by these factories has strained local jade supplies. Furthermore, the most prolific areas are already claimed, and unauthorized mining or collecting is strictly forbidden. Old gold-dredge tailings are currently being reworked for jade.

In an effort to conserve the resource, the New Zealand Parliament has passed an act forbidding the export of raw jade. Perhaps the best indication of the commercial shortage is reflected in the increasingly common recent practice of importing jade from elsewhere for carving in New Zealand. Conveniently, the nearest source of good nephrite is Australia; it is safe to say that any recent New Zealand carving in black jade had its origins in Australia.

Of course, an enormous amount of mining exploration has yet to be done in Australia, but fine nephrite has already been found in considerable amounts. In the early 1970s, for example, a deposit was discovered on the Eyre Peninsula, near Port Cowell on the western arm of the Spencer Gulf, in South Australia. Surveys proved the existence of significant reserves, and mining proceeded rapidly. By 1978, the operators claimed that they were supplying one quarter of the world's annual demand of 700 tons. New Zealand was the chief consumer of this nephrite, but large amounts were also exported to India, China, and the United States.

Jade Trade

Tracking the source of any jade that now appears on the market is no longer an easy task. Alaskan and British Columbian jades are commonly exported to the Orient, and quantities of Korean jade go to Taiwan, China, and Japan. Wyoming jade continues to be shipped in volume for cutting in China. Traffic in jade, in fact, has been extremely active and has almost no known boundaries, attesting to a universal interest in the material.

Taiwan offers a good example of how this trade can develop. Nephrite was found in the mountains about 20 kilometers southwest of Hualien (on the east coast of Taiwan) and 5 kilometers west of the town of Fengtien. Jade deposits occur in an east-to-northeast band that is approximately 2 miles wide by 6 miles long, between the Chiakang and Paipao Rivers. It occurs in beds or lenses associated, as usual, with serpentines and schists. The jade is bright green, yellowish green, or dull olive green; some is cat's-eye material. Bowenite is also found.

Original estimates indicated reserves as great as 800,000 metric tons. Although the area is somewhat isolated and travel is difficult, small-scale mining operations were begun as early as 1961. Within a matter of months, an instantly successful jade industry existed, with hundreds of small cutting shops specializing in bracelets, cabochons, and other commercial items. The demand for rough jade soon outstripped the supply, however, and the industry had to turn elsewhere for it. As a result, since 1963, Taiwan has been importing raw jade from British Columbia, India, and South Korea.

Korea offers a contrasting example of the international commerce in raw jade. Here, the nephrite comes from a single mine near Chunchon, about 20 miles south of the demilitarized zone between North and South Korea. The mine first opened as a talc mine, but this venture proved unprofitable for several reasons, one of which was the fact that jade mixed with the talc made the material difficult to crush and grind. Soon the mine was recognized as a source of fine, translucent nephrite that polished well and occurred in white to green colors, including some sea green and some brown. Despite the presence of this never-too-plentiful supply on its own soil, Korea never became known as a jade-cutting center because the bulk of it was exported to Japan and elsewhere for finishing.

Almost none of the rest of the world's reported jade deposits—such as the large talc-bearing nephrite deposit in the southern part of Grisons, Switzerland, in the Puschlav Valley—has had any significant impact on commerce or art. A steady trickle of jade continues from many minor sources into the noted stone cutting centers, but in the process, the material loses its identity and is tagged as Russian or Taiwanese or British Columbian or something else.

World Distribution of Jade

Sir Charles Hardinge, a noted British jade special-
ist and collector, published a list in 1961 of coun-
tries from which prehistoric, worked jade objects
have been reported. In introducing the list, he said,
"It is believed that the reports do not include objects carried there by later travelers, traders, whal-
ers, etc" (Hardinge 1961). By this he implied that
the native races themselves had worked the jade.
His list included:

Alaska	Loyalty Islands
Aleutian Islands	Marquesas
Asia Minor	Mexico
Assyria	New Caledonia
Austria	New Guinea
Babylonia	New Hebrides
Belgium	New Zealand
Brazil	Nicaragua
British Columbia	Panama
British Honduras	Peru
Burma	Philippines
Chatham Islands	Poland
China	Portugal
Columbia	Queen Charlotte Islands
Costa Rica	Saudi Arabia
Crete	Siberia
Eastern Turkestan	Sicily
Ecuador	Society Islands
El Salvador	Soviet Union
France	Spain
Germany	Sumatra
Great Britain	Switzerland
Greece	Syria
Guatemala	Tasmania
Guernsey	United States
India	Vancouver Island
Italy	Venezuela
Japan	West Indies
Korea	Yugoslavia

Obviously, any part of the world that has *not* had
contact with jade is conspicuous by its absence from
this far-ranging list.

FIVE

CHINA'S PRIZED STONE

So much has been published about Chinese jade carvings and so many beautiful carvings from the Orient have been exhibited that at the mere mention of jade many of us make an instant association with China. To separate the history and art of jade (as is attempted here) from the rest of China's artistic and cultural inheritance necessarily presents a somewhat skewed view of that inheritance. For the sake of balanced perspective, it is well to remember that China has an older tradition of work in pottery than in jade; moreover, a wealth of superb ceramics, bronzes, and other artifacts has been recovered, by comparison to which the quantity of jade is small.

Still, jade objects have been produced in China over a period of several thousand years in amounts sufficient to stuff all the world's major museums and innumerable private collections. Current excavations at archeological sites in China show very clearly that many more jade masterpieces remain buried, awaiting discovery. Since jade has always been highly prized in China and since its use spans time almost beyond measure, the objects recovered do constitute a nearly indestructible record of the ebb and flow of Chinese civilization—its changing philosophies and governments, and their effects on the activities of the people. It is interesting that the Chinese characters for king and jade are almost identical.

Origins of Carvings

Because jade carving is so intimately related to the sweep of Chinese history, scholars have tended to dwell on the sequence of production and the historical milieu of the carvings. This has been a formidable task because many of the objects studied were recovered by means of unscientific, uncontrolled excavations, by grave-robbing and the unlabeled accumulations in private collections. Only in the recent past has the export of old carvings from China finally been prohibited.

The problem is compounded by the existence of both innocent and planned fakery: each successive culture has copied from its predecessors. From the eleventh century onward, these reproductions have caused considerable trouble for collectors. As a case in point, examples are known of twelfth century A.D. carvings that are fine copies of carvings dating as far back as several centuries B.C. Even today, Hong Kong (and other) carvers are turning out

Probably worn as a hair ornament, this large (3¼-inch) phoenix with an unnaturally upright tail was carved of grayish-green and brown nephrite during the T'ang Dynasty (A.D. 618 to 906). Photo courtesy of the San Francisco Center of Asian Art and Culture.

"genuine antique" jade pieces as fast as they can get the raw materials. All of this activity, old and new, has come about because of the persistence of world interest in Chinese jade carvings for archeological, ethnological, and aesthetic reasons.

To the scholar who is attempting to trace the objects as historical entities, this state of affairs is very annoying; it can also be traumatic for the jade collector whose appreciation of a carving depends to any significant extent on its claimed pedigree. In the world of antique art, the pedigree of a piece often has more bearing on its market value than the carving's artistic quality does.

Timetable

Considering the difficulties involved, scholars have done a remarkable job of piecing together a history of China—at least in outline—through studies of pottery, bronzes, tombs, paintings, and some written records. Recent excavations on mainland China, undertaken in part to replace treasures that were removed from museums and collections and taken to Taiwan during the last great revolution, have refined this calendar somewhat; in general, however, they tend to support what was already known. The

The Chinese characters for jade, or yu. The old form (above) is very similar to the character for king; the current character for yu is below.

most striking feature of this history, given the succession of dynasties, feuding kingdoms, and emerging republics, is the overall unity of the culture—a culture that has changed slowly, over vast periods of time, under the influence of new imperial capitals and new philosophies. The modern reconstruction of China's calendar of history is shown in table 5-1 (making some allowance for honest differences among scholars).

Sources of Raw Jade

The evidence of the jade carvings produced in China over a minimum of 4,000 years may suggest that unending supplies of raw jade were conveniently at hand, but here the obvious turns out to be untrue. Jade in China has always been elusive, rare, and expensive, and its sources in nature lie far from

A cup with lid, standing slightly over 4 inches tall, carved of light green nephrite in seventeenth-century China. The surface relief carving mimics much earlier symbolic designs of an animal and bird in confrontation against a background grain pattern. Photo courtesy of the San Francisco Center of Asian Art and Culture.

The Chinese symbol for yu, *or jade.*

the cutting and carving centers. For most of the enormous span of history involved, the carvers of Peking and elsewhere relied on jade sources that were outside of China and over 2,000 miles away. It is miraculous that the jade culture could survive, let alone flourish, considering the incredible difficulties in getting the material.

The jade used was nephrite, and almost all of it came from the region near the cities of Khotan and Yarkand and on the slopes of the Kunlun Mountains in Eastern Turkestan. The best deposits were north of Kashmir, in what is now Sinkiang Uighur Autonomous Region. Khotan was an ancient trading center; sitting in the Khotan Oasis, it was surrounded on three sides by the Takla Makan Desert and on the fourth by the Kunlun Mountains. It was conquered by the Chinese in 73 A.D., fell to the Arab Kotaiba ibn Moslim from Western Turkestan in the eighth century, was destroyed by Ghengis Khan in

Table 5-1. Reconstruction of China's Dynastic Successions.*

Paleolithic period	600000 B.C. to 7000 B.C. (approx.)
Neolithic period	7000 B.C. to 1600 B.C. (approx.)
Shang Dynasty	1600 B.C. to 1027 B.C. (approx.)
Western Chou Dynasty	1027 B.C. to 771 B.C.
Period of spring and summer annals	770 B.C. to 475 B.C.
Period of the warring states	475 B.C. to 221 B.C.
(Kingdom of Tien)	300 B.C. to 100 B.C.
Ch'in Dynasty	221 B.C. to 207 B.C.
Western Han Dynasty	206 B.C. to A.D. 8
Hsin Dynasty (Wang Mang)	A.D. 9 to A.D. 23
Eastern Han Dynasty	A.D. 24 to A.D. 220
Period of the six dynasties	A.D. 220 to A.D. 580
Sui Dynasty	A.D. 581 to A.D. 618
T'ang Dynasty	A.D. 618 to A.D. 906
Five dynasties	A.D. 907 to A.D. 960
Sung Dynasty	A.D. 960 to A.D. 1279
(Liao Dynasty)	A.D. 916 to A.D. 1125
(Chin Dynasty)	A.D. 1115 to A.D. 1234
Yuan Dynasty	A.D. 1271 to A.D. 1368
Ming Dynasty	A.D. 1368 to A.D. 1644
Ching Dynasty	A.D. 1645 to A.D. 1912
Republic	A.D. 1912 to present

* Dates of dynasties occasionally overlap, indicating that two or more dynasties struggled for ascendancy until one triumphed. Dates noted in parentheses indicate that two dynasties struggled for power but both persisted.

1220, and was visited by Marco Polo in 1274—at which time it was again a thriving city. After centuries of alternating peace, revolt, and general turmoil, Eastern Turkestan became a province of China in the nineteenth century.

For 2,000 years Khotan has supplied jade to China. Much of the stone came from the beds of the two rivers watering the Khotan Oasis, the Karakash (Black Jade River) and the Yurung-kash (White Jade River); eventually in-place mining began in the Kunlun Mountains, where the two rivers originated. It has been reported that the only true white nephrite came from the Yurung-kash prior to the fifteenth century and that all "white" material found since that time has been tinged with green.

In the seventeenth century, activity shifted 200 miles to the northwest, to the city of Yarkand and its Zarafshan River. Probably the largest quantities found as river boulders came from the upper waters of the Tisnab River, 80 miles from Yarkand.

Nephrite from Sinkiang—whether recovered as river boulders or broken from the slopes of the Kunlun Mountains by lighting fires and then dousing the stone with water to crack it—was carried northwest to the marketing center of Kashgar. From this trading post, camel caravans made their way eastward. Some took the northern route that led across the great Gobi Desert and on into northern China. Others traveled southeast, skirting the Kunlun and Nan Shan mountains (where a little more jade was occasionally available), and thence moved eastward, meeting the caravan route from the north. The jade trade must have been extremely profitable to sustain the hauling of tons of rock over those vast distances by camel caravan for so many centuries.

East Turkestan remained the source of China's jade until the eighteenth century, during the reign of Emperor Ch'ien Lung. Jadeite appears not to have been available in any quantity or quality before that time in China proper or in any neighboring country except Burma. A small amount of jadeite reportedly came from the Kaskem Valley in Yarkand until the Chinese were eventually driven out. Other reports tell of a beautiful emerald-green nephrite *(fei ts'yu)* from Lantien on the borders of Shensi Province.

In any case, Chinese jade was synonymous with Turkestan jade until the importation of excellent jadeite from Burma began in Ch'ien Lung's time. Canton was the center of this new trade, although quantities of it were cut in the established centers at Shanghai and Peking. The new jade came largely

The blade of this 10-inch Shang Dynasty (1600 B.C. to 1027 B.C.) ceremonial dagger is carved of tan nephrite with localized green areas. Its bronze handle was clearly designed to be fastened to a wood handle to form a typical dagger-shaped axe. Photo courtesy of the San Francisco Center of Asian Art and Culture.

from Upper Burma, where it occurred as boulders in the beds of the Chindwin and Mogaung tributaries of the Irrawaddy River. Development of a trade in deep green nephrite from the Lake Baikal region of Russia and from the slopes of mountains in western Yunnan Province began at about the same time. After untold centuries, China had finally gained access to new sources of jade.

Ritual Jade Carvings

When regional organization was first instituted in China by Shang kings, around 1600 B.C., early jade tools had already been perfected and had even gained the status of ceremonial objects of esoteric meaning. Probably the best sources of information concerning early use of ceremonial jade objects are the three great written rituals: the *Chou li*, the *Li ki*, and the *I li*. Admittedly, the *Chou li* was not completed until as late as the Han Dynasty, but it is nonetheless as valid a handbook as we have of Chou times (about the tenth century B.C.). As it is, by the time the *Chou li* was published, much of the meaning of the ritual jades was already lost. Like most early Chinese writings, the ritual wastes little effort in describing or explaining anything that was commonplace to its authors. Consequently, centuries later it had become almost impossible to translate what was being said into descriptions of recognizable objects. The only hope has been a monumental effort to match the written word with the fruits of archeological digging.

Masterworks of Chinese Jade in the National Palace Museum, a publication of the National Palace Museum in Taipei, states that "old writings and catalogs on jade are limited to Lu Ta-lin's *K'ao-ku-t'u* and Lung Ta-yuan's *Ku-yu-t'u-p'u* from the Sung Dynasty, while from the Yuan Dynasty we have Chu Te-jun's *Ku-yu-t'u*. The objects of jade recorded in the works by Chu and Lu are, however, infinitesimally small in number, and the work by Lung, being an obvious forgery, is totally unsatis-

factory for use in authentication or explanation of jade objects. Ch'u Chung-jung first came out with his *Ku-yu-t'u-lu* in the Tao Kuang era (1821–1850) of the Ch'ing Dynasty, and afterward Wu Ta-ch'eng wrote the *Ku-yu-t'u-k'ao*'' (National Palace Museum 1969).

A mottled grayish-brown and -white nephrite blade, set in a bronze handle inlaid with turquoise. Obviously meant for ceremonial purposes, the 8⅜- by 3⅛-inch object dates from the late Shang Dynasty (1600 B.C. to 1027 B.C.). Photo courtesy of the Freer Gallery of Art, Washington, D.C.

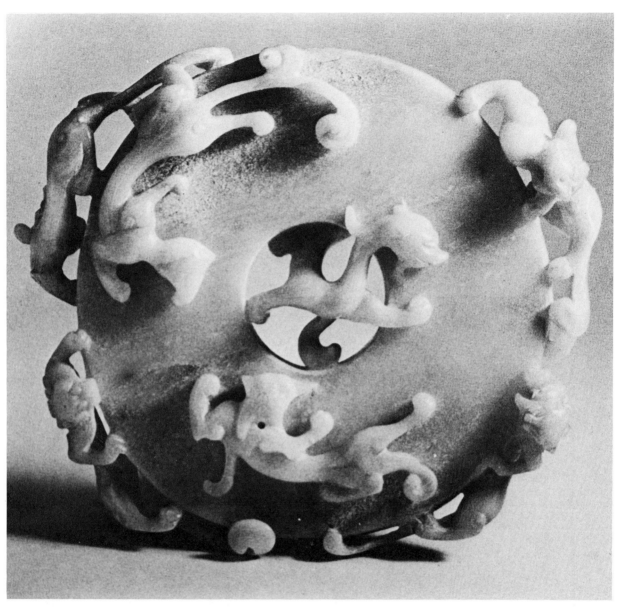

A pi-type disc with nine hydra, mystical beasts of the waters, looking like almost identical young dragons romping on its surface. This disc was whimsically but beautifully carved of bluish-gray nephrite during the Ming Dynasty (A.D. 1368 to 1644). Photo courtesy of the San Francisco Center of Asian Art and Culture.

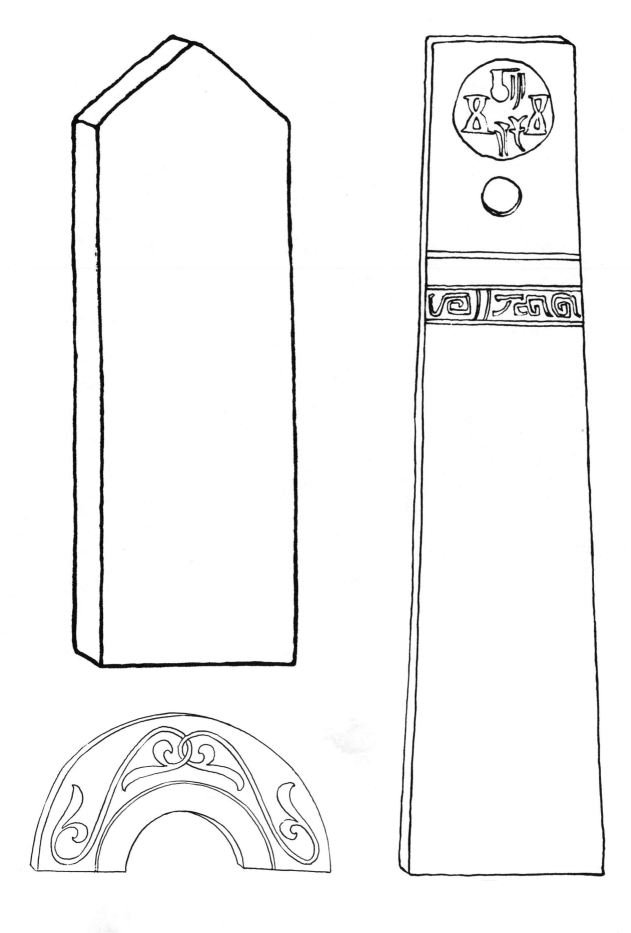

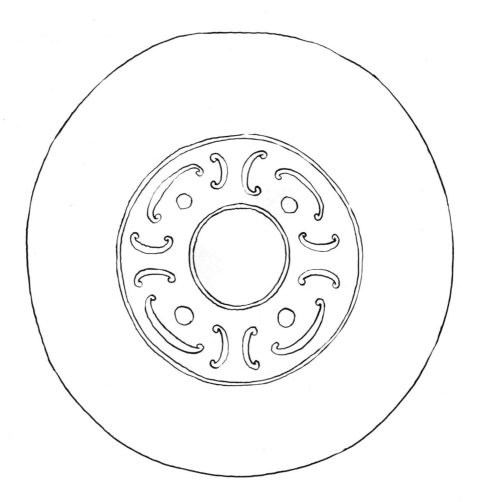

Forms of some of the ancient ritual jades, to which various meanings have been applied through many centuries.

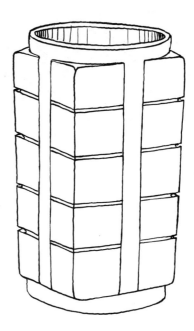

Perhaps the most important of the ritual jades that have persisted (at least in form) into our time are the six ritual jades mentioned in the *Chou li*. They are the *pi*, the *ts'ung*, the *kuei*, the *chang*, the *hu*, and the *huang*. The *pi* is a flat disk with a hole in the center. It came to symbolize Heaven and was blue-green in color. At burials, it became customary to place the *pi* under the body. The *ts'ung* is an open cylindrical tube whose outer surface is square in cross section—as if a hollow tube had been forced

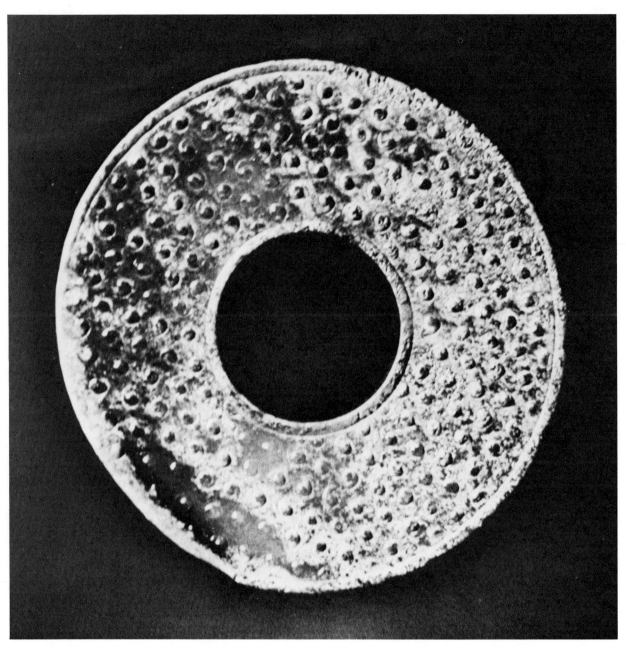

Very old, partially altered pi *(approximately 3½ inches), carved front and back with the traditional grain pattern. Of yellowish-brown nephrite, it dates from the late Chou Dynasty (700 or 800 B.C.). Photo courtesy of the Freer Gallery of Art, Washington, D.C.*

A Chou Period (1027 B.C. to 771 B.C.) ts'ung *of brownish nephrite. The unusual humanlike masks may also be a form of the* t'ao t'ieh, *or monster motif. Photo courtesy of the San Francisco Center of Asian Art and Culture.*

through a rectangular block. It became symbolic of the Earth and was yellow (perhaps to suggest the yellow clays of parts of China). At burials, it was placed on the chest of the body so that the corpse would lie between *pi* and *ts'ung*. The *kuei* is flat and blade-shaped, normally tapering to a point at one end. It became symbolic of wood and was always green. The *chang* is apparently a rod with one pointed end, but no actual description of it exists beyond its mention in ancient writings. Being symbolic of fire, it was red in color. The *hu* is usually represented as being in the form of a tiger. It came to symbolize metal and was required to be white. The *huang* is of somewhat uncertain description, too, but seemingly was semicircular and looked like half a *pi*. It became symbolic of water and was black.

For ritual or sacrificial purposes, the *pi* represented reverence to Heaven, the *ts'ung* reverence to Earth, the *kuei* reverence to the East, the *chang* reverence to the South, the *hu* reverence to the West, and the *huang* reverence to the North. These are undoubtedly not the original ritualistic meanings and uses for the six forms, some of which are in fact suspected of being phallic symbols. By Shang and Chou times, however, the meanings given above had become entrenched, and the forms had essentially stabilized. The following 3,000 years were to see the meanings embellished (and obscured) still further, even as the forms persisted with little variation in design.

Carved in mottled green and brown nephrite, this 4¼-inch ts'ung *dates from the Chou Dynasty (1027 B.C. to 771 B.C.) and is a classic example of this ancient ritual form. Photo courtesy of the Freer Gallery of Art, Washington, D.C.*

SIX

CHINESE SYMBOLISM

Yang and Yin, the Five Elements, and the *Pa Kua*

By early Shang times (1600 B.C.), astrology, astronomy, and numerology were already well established as means of divining the will of the gods and of prognosticating natural events such as weather, flood, drought, epidemics, and even political events such as wars and changes in government. Numerological systems in particular had attained incredible complexity. Most of the information about these systems has been lost but some of their symbolism is preserved in jade carvings that have defied the ravages of time.

A resurgence of interest in them has led to recent attempts at deciphering some of the meaning. For example, a paper published in *Scientific American* has proposed a solution for the meaning of the *Pa Kua,* a set of eight triad diagrams consisting of combinations of long and short bars (Gardner 1974). These eight sets are arranged in a circle in such an order that each is an inverse of the symbol opposite. These symbols have been used repeatedly on jade carvings for many centuries and their function seems to be to link the yang-yin principle of opposites with the five elements.

The yang and yin principles constitute one of the pillars of Chinese Taoism, which itself originated as a rather pure form of nature worship developed from observation of the procession of natural events. Eventually the religion became encrusted with numerous deities, much symbolism, and various rules of behavior, and still later it absorbed many of the external characteristics of Buddhism. In essence it now espouses effortless action, and its highest estate—freedom from desire and from sensory experience—can be attained only through mystical contemplation.

The yang and yin principles are an expression of the dual nature of creation and the universe. The yang principle is characterized as positive and male, and it is identified with the Sun. The Yin principle is negative, female, and Moon-oriented. Thus they represent the fundamental opposites that, acting through the five elements or five ancients (water, metal, fire, wood, earth), were said to have produced all things. The five elements were also considered to be the spirits of the five planets (Mercury, Venus, Mars, Jupiter, and Saturn), which in communion with the Sun and the Moon constituted the seven governors of all worldly affairs.

The fact that the yang and yin symbols sometimes accompany carvings of the eight signs of the *Pa Kua* supports the idea that a duality of causes or powers was thought to act through the five elements. The *Pa Kua* design interestingly resembles the standard model of the atom sketched out by physicist Neils Bohr, which is basic to our conception of the material universe. The numerology of the atom is no less complex and obscure than that of the *Pa Kua.*

Stems and Branches

Two other sets of ancient symbols recur frequently in Chinese jade carvings and indeed establish the form of the Chinese calendar itself. These are the ten celestial stems and the twelve terrestrial branches. The stems are closely related to the five elements: the element Metal has the stems for Metallic Ore and Kettles, the element Water those for Fresh and Salt water, the element Fire those for Lightning and Burning Incense, the element Earth those for Hills and Earthenware, and the element Wood those for Trees and Cut Timber.

The twelve terrestrial branches correspond to what we would call the twelve signs of the zodiac and likewise arose from the study of the stars. The list of constellations differs from ours in being composed wholly of real or imaginary animals. In proper order, the branches are those of the Rat, the Ox, the Tiger, the Hare, the Dragon, the Serpent, the Horse, the Goat, the Monkey, the Cock, the Dog, and the Boar. Although (strangely) the ten celestial stems do not appear with any frequency in carvings, the twelve terrestrial branches are often seen. Possibly this is due to the great emphasis animal forms had been given in carvings dating from the earliest (pre-Shang) Taoist times.

Ancient Chinese writings have pushed the date of combination of the stems and branches as far back as 2700 B.C.; if so, as many as 2,500 years elapsed before the combination was first used, during the Han Dynasty, for numbering years. Under this system, the ten stems were listed in a column that repeated them six times; to the left of this column, the twelve branches were listed in a column that repeated them five times. Thus sixty unique binomial branch-stem pairs representing sixty years were created. Although the sixty-year cycle was not adopted for the Chinese calendar until Han times (just before the beginning of the Christian era in the West), combinations of the symbols are known on carvings of a much earlier date.

Ancient Ornaments and Designs

There is still another set of carving decorations whose origins are lost in antiquity. In the *She King*, an important work dating from the Sung Dynasty in about A.D. 1000, the twelve *chang* or ancient ornaments were revived after centuries of disuse. Unfortunately, although these were mentioned in publications antedating the Sung period, they were not illustrated and their revival was consequently based on the Sung conception of what they must be.

In a rough translation, the Sung Emperor Shun is reported to say of these ornaments,

> I wish to see the emblematic figures of the ancients, the Sun, the Moon, the stars, the mountains, the dragon, and the flowery fowl, which are depicted on the upper garment; the temple cups, the aquatic grass, the flames, the grains of rice, the hatchet, and the symbol of distinction, which are embroidered on the lower garment; I wish to see all of these displayed with the five colors, so as to form the official robes (Williams 1960).

At that stage the twelve ornaments may have been restricted to decorations for official robes, but in time they predictably appeared together or singly as the subjects of ceremonial jade carvings.

The list of designs and themes for decorating carvings grew longer through the centuries. Buddhist symbols (including the eight happy omens and the seven gems), Taoist symbols (including the eight immortals, the hundred antiques, and the eight precious things), and a host of miscellaneous symbols (including the swastika) were pressed into use. The swastika is an emblem of great antiquity; in China, under the influence of Buddhism, it came to symbolize the doctrines of Buddha and eventually the Heart of Buddha.

Without doubt, China's most often-repeated carving design through the ages has been the very ancient *t'ao t'ieh*. This malevolent-looking face, which has come to be known as the monster design, is a grotesque and crude mask with two big round eyes and a missing lower jaw. Large tusks protrude from the upper jaw giving it a ferocious and beastlike appearance; each side of the nose bears an incurving horn. From under the eyes, two bands usually rise at right angles and end in a tail; below each band, a set of claws can often be seen.

Dr. S. W. Bushell, a student of Chinese art in the early 1900s, spoke of the *t'ao t'ieh* as follows: "The gluttonous ogre with a fang projecting on each side no doubt figures the all-devouring storm god of the Chinese..." (Bushell, quoted in Laufer 1974). Actually, considerable scholarly doubt remains about what the figure represents, but there is no doubt that

A group of bats carved in gray-green nephrite with brown markings, made during the late Ming or early Ch'ing dynasties. The bat was a symbol of happiness and it is suggested that the five bats here represent the five blessings—riches, long life, peace, virtue, and a natural death. Photo courtesy of the San Francisco Center of Asian Art and Culture.

A large (almost 15 inches in diameter), translucent, spinach-green nephrite bowl. T'ao t'ieh, or monster figure masks, are prominent, as are the always amazing loose-ring carvings. The bowl dates from the early Ch'ing Dynasty (about A.D. 1650). Photo courtesy of the Smithsonian Institution, Washington, D.C.

it is pre-Shang in origin and that it is of prime significance in the origins of Taoism. By the time of the Shang Dynasty, the *t'ao t'ieh* began to appear on carvings as a complex design formed by parts of two or more of four very ancient and important creature designs: the dragon *(lung)*, the phoenix *(feng-huang)*, the unicorn *(chi-lin)*, and the tortoise *(shen-kuei)*. Of these four, perhaps the creature that intrigues the imagination most, as it romps and slithers its way through thousands of years of history and tons of carvings, is the dragon.

In Western cultures, the dragon is a winged reptilian beast with lion claws, eagle wings, serpent tail, and fiery breath. This conception is found in many places on the Earth and has persisted since Babylonian times. In general, the dragon of the West is considered a dangerous, evil, and rapacious beast to be hated, feared, and (on occasion), slaughtered. Even so, it is the national symbol of Wales, acts as an essential character in many stories, and was second only to the eagle as a symbol for the Romans.

The Chinese attitude toward the dragon has been

quite different. To them, it was a beast signifying many things benevolent, worthy, and powerful. The consensus of scholars is that the dragon represents various cosmic forces, a view that accounts both for its importance and for the fact that Chinese dragons appear in forms and designs as changeable and numerous as the different kinds of forces represented. A very ancient Chinese description insists that dragons have the head of a camel, the eyes of a devil, the horns of a deer, the ears of a cow, the neck of a snake, the scales of a carp, the belly of a frog, the claws of an eagle, and the feet of a tiger. Through the centuries, considerable artistic liberty has been taken with these features, including the frequent addition of two pairs of wings and even of flowing masses of hair.

Then, too, the conception and form of the dragon were bound to change considerably when Taoism itself (in which the creature had its origins) was shaken and altered by the times of political instability following the fall of the Han Dynasty and by the impact of the teachings of Buddhism. Professor

Many of the larger nephrite objects of the Ch'ing Dynasty, like this 18-inch hu, *or vaselike wine vessel, were carved of dark, spinach-colored jade. Modeled after earlier bronze forms, this vessel's major feature is its large t'ao t'ieh, or monster mask. Photo courtesy of the San Francisco Center of Asian Art and Culture.*

An early seventeenth-century Chinese drinking cup with black and brown markings over greenish-gray nephrite. Over 10 inches tall, the cup is dominated by an oddly shaped but aggressive-looking feng-huang, or phoenix (one of the four supernatural creatures), which seems to be growing out of the cup rather than merely clinging to it. Photo courtesy of the San Francisco Center of Asian Art and Culture.

A pair of carp (7¼ inches) transmuting into dragons, carved of deep green and brown nephrite during the Ch'ing Dynasty (late 1800s). The change from carp to dragon, under special circumstances, was part of the accepted lore of China. Photo courtesy of the San Francisco Center of Asian Art and Culture.

Very old dragon pendant (5¼ inches long) carved of partially weathered greenish nephrite. Dating from the time of the Warring States (475 B.C. to 221 B.C.), it was probably originally an inset for a large metal belt hook. Photo courtesy of the San Francisco Center of Asian Art and Culture.

d'Argence, a prominent student of oriental art, described the change Chinese dragons had undergone in the 1,700 years since Han times:

> These sturdy animals differ from the lithe, wiry, and disheveled creatures of former times. They are more stately, more earthly, also more imposing, almost menacing. With their square shoulders, their paws planted firmly on the ground (or on the clouds) and their enormous mouths showing bare teeth, they seem to be in a perpetual posture of combat. Eighteenth-century [Chinese] dragons are usually equipped with two-pointed antlers, bifurcated manes, voluminous beards, and interminable whiskers with spiraling extremities (d'Argence 1972).

In whatever form, the dragon persisted and has become the most familiar motif in all Chinese art.

Motifs from Nature

From the beginning of the Han Dynasty onward, carvings of animals and plants of the nature-oriented religion were ubiquitous. Practically every running, creeping, swimming, crawling, or flying creature known to the Chinese came into service in some symbolic sense and as a theme for the jade carver. Plants, fruits, and flowers were used the same way except that fewer were venerated to the same degree that members of the animal kingdom were. It was during Han times that small carved animal forms were introduced as grave pieces to be placed with the body as guardians and symbols. Eventually, small jade amulets were placed at all body openings because of the widespread belief that jade was preventive against putrefaction. A small cicada amulet, for example, was considered essential as a tongue or mouth piece.

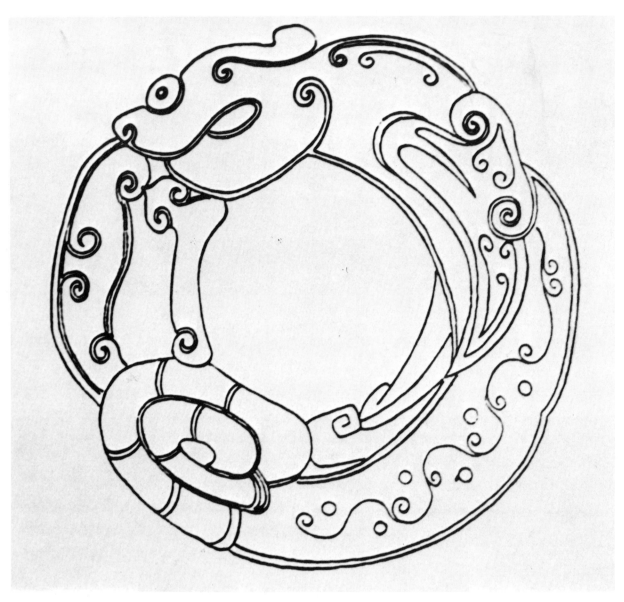

As recorded in this sketch, the dragon passed through various phases of depiction in China, from a recognizable mythical beast to geometric abstractions.

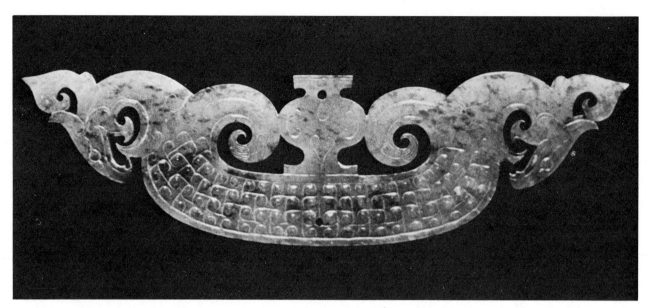

A 4½-inch-long flat nephrite ornament, terminating in two stylized dragon heads and ornamented with a grain pattern. Dates from the late Chou Dynasty (1027 B.C. to 771 B.C.). Photo courtesy of the Freer Gallery of Art, Washington, D.C.

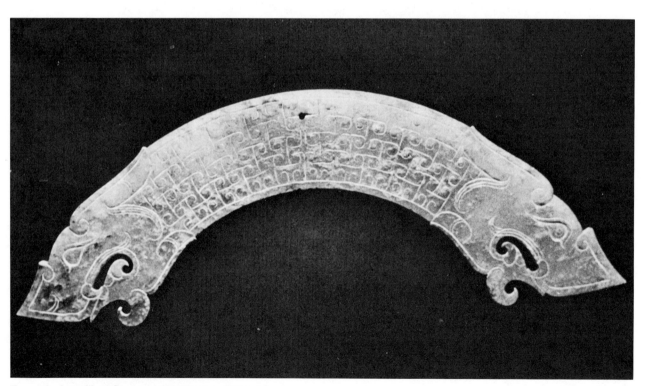

From the late Chou Dynasty (1027 B.C. to 771 B.C.), a two-headed, stylized dragon balances a nephrite ornament perforated for hanging. Photo courtesy of the Freer Gallery of Art, Washington, D.C.

Pale green and waxy looking, a particularly imposing dragon dominates this eighteenth-century nephrite carving. The virtuosity of the Chinese artist-carver is obvious, not only in the fine finish, complexity, and balance of the piece but in the unusual depth and open work of the carving, which is hollow in the center. Photo courtesy of the San Francisco Center of Asian Art and Culture.

Ornament carved with two dragons so highly stylized as to be almost unnoticeable at first glance. From the late Chou Dynasty (1027 B.C. to 771 B.C.), the ornament is carved of nephrite that has turned from light tan to gray from decomposition. Photo courtesy of the Freer Gallery of Art, Washington, D.C.

An exhibition of recent Chinese archeological finds has been presented in the West by the People's Republic of China. Among the pieces in it is the famous jade burial suit of Princess Tou Wan. The show's catalog states:

> Taoist . . . lore included a belief that jade could prevent the decay of the corpse which therefore, from about the time of the Man'ch'eng tombs, was often furnished with small jade pieces intended to stop the nine orifices of the body, a cicada of jade being laid upon the tongue. Prince Li and his wife took this belief to ostentatious length and prepared for themselves complete suits of jade, being perhaps the instigators of a fashion which was still observed occasionally in later times. Lady Tou's suit consisted of 2,160 tablets of jade varying in size from 4½ by 3½ to 1½ by 1 centimeters and .2 to .35 centimeters in thickness. The suit divides into twelve parts . . . made as separate units with piping of silk-wound iron wire along the edges. The remaining stitching is with gold wire passed through holes at the corners of the tablets, except across the chest, where the jade tablets are held in place by adhesive attaching their binding tapes to the heavy cloth lining. The decayed tapes have had to be replaced. The jade was probably imported from Sinkiang. Western Han Dynasty: late 2nd century B.C. (Watson 1973).

The bat and butterfly were two particularly popular winged creatures among the Han animals. In time, several centuries from the date of their introduction during the Han Dynasty, both became so symbolic and stylized that it is sometimes difficult to distinguish a very ornate bat from a butterfly—as, for example, when a butterfly is given disklike wings, the body of a cicada, and antennae that

Realistic Ming Dynasty (A.D. 1368 to 1644) carving of a rodent, made of spotted, greenish-brown nephrite. Photograph by Lee Boltin.

Ornate tiger of tan and mottled green nephrite (3 inches long). Now partially discolored from alteration, the carving has remained clear and distinct since its fashioning during the Chou Dynasty (1027 B.C. to 771 B.C.). Photo courtesy of the Freer Gallery of Art, Washington, D.C.

A gray-green and brown nephrite standing bear, in a more human than bearlike pose. Although this piece was carved in about the third to sixth centuries A.D., it suggests the more natural animal forms to be carved in the distant future. Photo courtesy of the San Francisco Center of Asian Art and Culture.

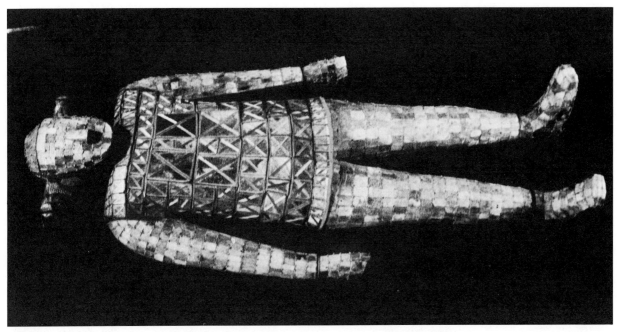

*A 1968 excavation of Princess Tou Wan's tomb at Man-ch'eng, China, yielded her jade
burial suit, composed of 2,160 nephrite tablets. She and her husband, Prince Liu Sheng,
demonstrated their strong belief in the lore that jade could prevent the decay of
corpses. Approximately 5 feet 8 inches long, the suit was made for the Princess in the
late second century B.C.*

spread into stems, leaves, and peach blossoms. The combination of the bat and butterfly in a carving was much approved in China because the butterfly traditionally symbolized immortality (as it did for the Greeks) and the bat represented long life and happiness. Some significance, of course, attaches to the fact that the Chinese word *fu-i,* depending on its pronunciation, may mean either ''bat'' or ''happiness.''

The bat was further distinguished during the Han Dynasty as being one of five animals endowed with planetary powers. Its four companions were the deer, the lion, the eagle, and the fish, all of which appear with considerable frequency in jade carvings. Among other things, the deer was credited with being the only animal able to find the sacred fungus of long life (with which it is often depicted); this idea followed from the fact that deer were believed to live for centuries and thus became a symbol of longevity.

The lion first appeared in Chinese carving no earlier than the Han Dynasty, when it was introduced with Buddhism from India. Generally, the lion in stone assumed the role of guardian and was used at entrances to Buddhist temples. During Ming Dynasty times, particular emphasis was given to a conventionalized form known as the lion dog of Fo; this lion, playing with a ball symbolizing the law, is the customary temple guardian. The winged lion, which seems to have been introduced about the sixth century A.D., also appears regularly in carvings.

Considerable confusion seems to have existed among carvers, apparently, in differentiating between the lionlike *ch'i-lin,* or unicorn, and the newly introduced Buddhist lion; this produced the third common lionlike figure, the chimera, which looks like a muddled combination of lion and unicorn and has been described as resembling a lion with a dragonlike head. Actually, carvers employed considerable artistic license in creating a wide variety of these chimeras, but the carvings all show a definite kinship to lions. On the other hand, many lion carvings have distinctly dragonlike features. Seemingly, the carver was frequently tempted artistically to stray from the requirements of ritual and to mix animal forms in pursuit of aesthetic satisfaction.

Details of the jade burial suit of Princess Tou Wan, showing how the jade plates of the arm, head, leg, and foot sections were stitched together with imperishable gold wire. The reconstructed chest section shows how this separate part—one of twelve sections— had a piping of silk-covered iron wire.

Buddhist Influence

While many of the plant and animal forms of Chinese carving can be definitely traced to their Taoist origins, they were certainly affected by the grafting of Buddhism onto the ancient nature religion. For example, Taoism inspired the duck, symbol of happy marriage; the goose, conveying the same meaning; the crane, messenger of the gods; the fox, guardian of buried treasure and bearer of the souls of the dead; the three-legged toad, symbol of the unattainable; and the peach, most common symbol of immortality. When Buddhism arrived in China, at approximately the middle of Han times, it gradually altered the meanings and forms of all

these Taoist symbols—as well as introducing its own.

The lotus is the most widely used and revered Buddhist symbol. To a Buddhist, the lotus represents purity and perfection, two fundamental objectives of the religion. The endless cycle of petals symbolizes beautifully the idea of constantly recurring cycles of reincarnation. By the Tang Dynasty (ninth century A.D.), the lotus—as a whole, in various parts, and in cross sections—was appearing in carvings.

Still another basic design, the clockwise swastika and the counterclockwise suavastika, was likely adopted by Buddhism from Hinduism and carried by Buddhists into China. By Ming and Ching times, both forms were in frequent use as a very auspi-

A dark green 15-inch marriage bowl from the late Ming Dynasty (A.D. 1368 to 1644). The bat handles symbolize happiness, and the peony bouquet in the bowl is a sign of spring and new beginnings as well as happiness and love. Photo courtesy of the Smithsonian Institution, Washington, D.C.

cious, lucky symbol. Similarly the mystic knot, or knot of everlasting happiness, was seldom seen before Ming times but became popular during the resurgence of jade carving under the later Ching emperors.

The motif of a pair of fishes—although firmly established as one of the eight auspicious signs from the Footprint of Buddha, and therefore obviously of Buddhist orientation—seems to have originated in Han times, before Buddhism arrived (Williams 1960). Aside from their auspicious significance, the paired fish signify marital happiness and frequently adorn wedding gifts.

The marriage of Taoism and Buddhism has produced some rather remarkable combinations. For example, the traditional Buddhist prayer wheel, when carved in jade, may have a central movable button that, when held between thumb and forefinger, permits the small flat outer wheel to be revolved with the other hand. The outer wheel may depict lotus petals or the bats of happiness or the marks of the *Pa Kua* or butterflies or dragons or any other combination of Taoist and Buddhist symbols. The center button may bear the yang-yin design, the swastika, the longevity symbol, or some other basic design. Thus, aesthetic and religiously meaningful combinations were available in unlimited quantities to the carver.

The bat, standing for long life and happiness, has appeared in a great variety of forms in Chinese carving, but most frequently head-down with obvious wings and rodent ears.

The flowers of the citrus medica look so fingerlike that they became known as Buddha's fingers. This carving (8 inches long), of gray-green nephrite with brown markings, dates from the Ming Dynasty (A.D. 1368 to 1644). Photo courtesy of the San Francisco Center of Asian Art and Culture.

Human Symbols

By far the most important effect of Buddhism on jade carving was its encouragement of the gradual introduction of deities in the form of human figures. Some small, highly stylized but recognizable human figures had indeed appeared as far back as 1000 B.C., during the Chou Dynasty, but Taoist deities are not known to have been personified as natural human figures until about the seventeenth century (Ming Dynasty).

The fact that Taoism tended to keep its deities abstract and represented only by symbols must have had some bearing on the lack of figure carvings. Buddha, however, was definitely human and his close associates were, too; so even though the principles of the religion might remain abstract, the holiest of its teachers had human form.

Once the trend of carving human forms began, it rapidly gained popularity and was done in great style. Sacred individuals were numerous, and all were portrayed in jade. Among the most popular subjects were the *pah sien* or eight immortals:

Chung-li Ch'uan, leader of the eight immortals, dwelt on the Mountain of Jade and became immortal through being perfectly attuned to nature. He is carved as a fat, bearded, half-naked little man carrying a fan and a peach, or fungus (symbol of immortality).

Lu Tung-pin, who is carved as an older man in scholar's costume, carries a magic sword and is revered as the protector of magicians and a doer of magical deeds.

Chang Kuo-lao, a famous magician, is often carved as riding a donkey—sometimes backward—and always as carrying the *yu ku*, a kind of tubular drum.

Ts'ao Kuo-chiu, the most recent of the immortals, is usually portrayed as bearded and dressed in beautiful robes, with a hat or cap; he is never seen without a pair of clapperlike castanets in his hand.

Han Hsiang-tzu is obviously a musician and is always seen playing his magic flute.

A tiny (1⅞ inch), almost robot-looking Chou Dynasty (1027 B.C. to 771 B.C.) demon mask carved of highly translucent light green nephrite. Photo courtesy of the Freer Gallery of Art, Washington, D.C.

An archaic yellowish-green nephrite carving of a man, dating from the Han Dynasty (206 B.C. to A.D. 220). Standing slightly over 3 inches tall, this piece illustrates the avoidance of reality in Chinese human-figure carving, which was not to change until many centuries later. Photo courtesy of the San Francisco Center of Asian Art and Culture.

Ho Hsien-ku, the only certain woman among the immortals, joined the select group of eight by consuming one of the magic peaches of immortality; the stemmed lotus flower is her emblem.

Li T'ieh-kuai, always shown as a crippled beggar carrying a crutch, returned in spirit too late from the Celestial Regions to prevent his empty body from being destroyed and so (hastily) had to enter the body of a dying beggar; the body thereupon became his own for the rest of his earthly life.

Lan Ts'ai-ho, traditionally dressed as a woman in a blue gown, is said to have wandered the streets, singing songs about the joys of immortality; he or she (the sex is not certain, but legend seems to favor ''he'') is always depicted as carrying a basket of flowers and often has one foot resting on a spade.

Artist's conception of Chung-li Ch'uan, leader of the eight immortals.

Artist's conception of Lu Tung-pin, scholar and protector of magicians, another of the eight immortals.

Artist's conception of Chang Kuo-lao, the magician, one of the eight immortals.

Artist's conception of Ts'ao Kuo-chiu, patron of the theater and the most recent of the eight immortals.

Artist's conception of Han Hsiang-tzu, flute-playing patron of musicians, one of the eight immortals.

Artist's conception of Ho Hsien-ku, one of the eight immortals, who became such by eating the peach of immortality.

Artist's conception of Li T'ieh-kuai, the crippled beggar, one of the eight immortals.

Artist's conception of Lan Ts'ai-ho, the troubadour who sang of the joys of immortality, one of the eight immortals.

Shakyamuni Buddha (10 inches) in obvious meditation, carved with great sensitivity and balance of pale green nephrite during the late Ch'ing Dynasty (late 1800s). Photo courtesy of the San Francisco Center of Asian Art and Culture.

The chop, *or official seal, of reigning emperor Ch'ien Lung (*A.D. *1736 to 1795) of the Ch'ing Dynasty. Many jade pieces produced by his carving shops carry the seal, as do a number of counterfeit carvings worked in later times.*

The popular figures of these eight immortals and that of Lao-tzu, the founder of organized Taoism who was born about 600 B.C., were inspired by Taoism. To this group, Buddhism added its own gallery of personalities. Buddha himself was depicted in so many attitudes and gestures that art historians have classified them by category. *Shakyamuni* (The Lord Buddha), *Maitreya* (The Laughing Buddha), *Ananda* (The Teacher and Disciple), and the Eighteen *Lohans* [Buddhist saints] have all been abundantly portrayed.

In the west, however, the most popular of the Buddhist figures are the elegant statuettes of the character known as Kuan Yin. This female personage, usually carved as graceful, serene, and gentle, is one of the *Bodhisattvas*—individuals who reached the peak of spiritual perfection under Buddhism but spurned the final reward to stay behind and help other human beings. Kuan Yin holds a position of special affection and is even believed by some to represent the asexual reincarnation of the future *Buddha Avalokitesvara* (The Compassionate Buddha). Kuan Yin was already being venerated as a kind of protective goddess in the sixth century A.D.; by 1700, under Jesuit influence, she was even

being represented as something like a madonna with child. Other *Bodhisattvas,* including *Samantabhadra* seated on the back of an elephant and *Minjusri* seated on a lion, have never achieved comparable popularity.

European Influence

The Han Dynasty and the introduction of Buddhism obviously had a profound effect on jade carving. Contact with Europe and with Western culture by the time of the Ming Dynasty in the 1600s and on into the Ching Dynasty in the 1700s had a similar effect. Commerce with Europe coincided with an extended period of internal political stability, fostering a new standard of perfection in jade carving. With the advent of a series of powerful, intelligent, cultured emperors, the ancient arts of China flourished. No other carvings approach the achievements of stone-cutting artists during the sixty-year reign of Emperor Ch'ien Lung, from 1736 to 1795. As stated by Stanley Charles Nott, "The quality of the nephrite and jadeite used by the carvers was the finest; no fever of haste held the craftsmen in its grip, and the minutest detail was not forgotten; the finished carving had of necessity to be the finest that human skill could produce—commerce had not yet infected this branch of art with its destructive stimulant" (Nott 1962).

The distinguishing characteristic of carvings of the Ching Dynasty is that artists were more interested in producing decorative objects than in copying the archaic jades. More and more they became occupied with making vases, statuettes, candleholders, brush holders, and other fine decorative pieces for wealthy patrons. During Emperor Ch'ien Lung's reign, the peak of productivity and perfection was reached. Jade carvings of the period bear little resemblance to the early ceramics, bronzes, or the ceremonial burial jades; they are more suggestive of magnificent European sculptures, while remaining totally Chinese in conception and making flamboyant use of all the old symbolism. These works remain the top show pieces of jade in all the world's great museums.

Many ancient bronze forms were reproduced in jade, sometimes exactly and sometimes with embellishments and modifications. Incense burners, the *ting* (a four-legged casket), the *ku* (an open flaring spill vase), the *kuang* (a ewer), candlespikes, bowls in open or covered forms, statuary, joss stick hold-

This 9-inch kuang, *or wine vessel, carved of deep green nephrite during the Ch'ing Dynasty (A.D. 1645 to 1912), was worked in imitation of earlier bronze* kuang *forms. Photo courtesy of the Smithsonian Institution, Washington, D.C.*

ers, circular or rectangular table screens, miniature landscaped mountains peopled with legendary characters, double-cylindric honorific vases, boxes and covers, the *ju-i* (a scepter), cylindrical *lien* (scroll holders), and wine vessels of various sorts were all part of the jade carvers' repertoire.

Carvings frequently measured over a foot tall. Lids, chains, and rings were commonly used for embellishment and—in an amazing show of technical skill—were often carved in place, along with the main object, from the same piece of jade. The tough-

ness of jade permitted carvers to work with it without fear of breakage, as if it were a highly plastic substance, and they took utmost advantage of this characteristic. So intense was Ch'ien Lung's interest in jade carvings that reportedly he even had in his imperial workshops a special section called the *Hsi Fan Tso* (Indian School) responsible for producing jade carvings in the Indian style, with very delicate and graceful designs and sometimes with jewel settings.

A pair of 10-inch perforated cap stands with white nephrite tops and inlays of other white nephrite pieces. These were among the many extraordinary carvings removed from the Chinese Summer Palace during the 1859 Boxer Rebellion. Photo courtesy of the Smithsonian Institution, Washington, D.C.

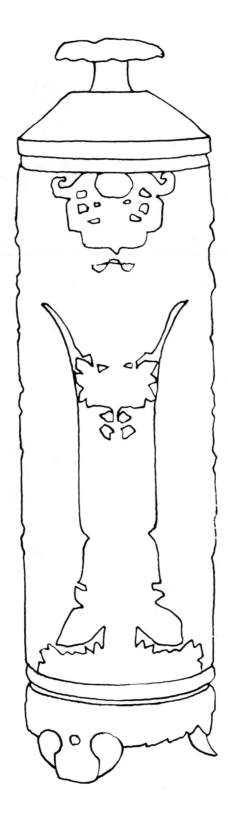

Typical examples of earlier Chinese bronze forms copied in jade, often with considerable embellishment.

A pair of 10-inch perforated cap stands with white nephrite tops and inlays of other white nephrite pieces. These were among the many extraordinary carvings removed from the Chinese Summer Palace during the 1859 Boxer Rebellion. Photo courtesy of the Smithsonian Institution, Washington, D.C.

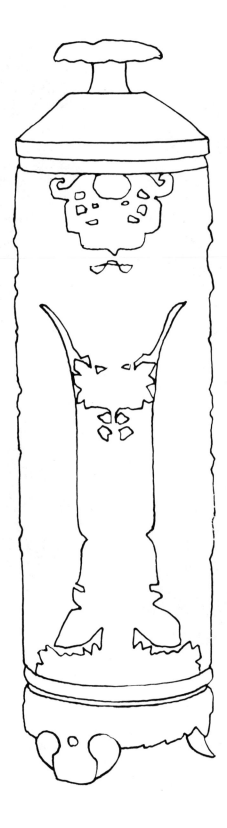

Typical examples of earlier Chinese bronze forms copied in jade, often with considerable embellishment.

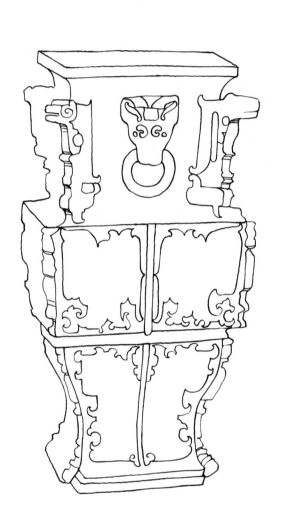

Distribution of Ching Dynasty Carvings

The presence of so many fine Ch'ien Lung pieces in Western museums and private collections is due to a series of actions taken by the Western powers against China toward the end of the Ching Dynasty. In the second half of the nineteenth century, the Western powers had developed extensive commercial interests in China. To protect their interests, French and British troops became engaged in military action. In the process, they sacked the Imperial Summer Palace in Peking in 1860, making off with many of its treasures and driving out the Manchu emperor. During this time, the T'ai P'ing rebellion was launched against the Dynasty. To preserve their own status, the Western powers supported the now-subservient imperial family and put down the rebellion. The dowager Empress Tz'u Hsi had appointed a nephew, Kwang Hsu, as Emperor. He, in turn, formulated a number of changes intended to adopt Western customs and thereby strengthen China. The dowager Empress objected, forced his abdication, and encouraged a rebellion to return to the old ways.

In retaliation for the new attacks on their special privileges and on their foreign enclaves, the Western powers crushed the so-called Boxer Rebellion, thereby opening China to the West and releasing a new supply of Chinese treasures to the European market. Many specimens that survived the T'ai P'ing looting, as well as other pieces scattered elsewhere in China, were eventually sold to dealers and collectors in the West during subsequent periods of political and economic chaos.

During the final great Chinese revolution of our times, when the Nationalist government and troops fled to Taiwan, they carried with them an enormous quantity of cultural treasure—ceramics, bronzes, jade carvings, and so on. These pieces, though relatively unknown to Westerners, are now housed in the National Palace Museum in Taipei. The museum's curators maintain that its collection of jade objects is unmatched by any other collection, public or private, in the world. The very existence of such a fine collection (and it *is* as good as they say) is a testimony to the esteem the Chinese continue to accord the symbols of their cultural heritage. It is also a measure of the quantity and quality of the jade objects produced through several millenia that so many superb pieces have been preserved and are still in Chinese hands despite the great cultural and political upheavals China has experienced in its long history.

SEVEN

JADE IN THE NEW WORLD

New Appreciation

To enjoy the pottery, bronzes, and stone carvings of ancient Chinese, Egyptian, Indian, or Roman culture, an admirer need merely make a pilgrimage to one of the great art museums of the world. Until relatively recent times, however, anyone wishing to study the glorious artifacts of the Inca, Olmec, Mayan, Aztec, or other ancient Central American civilizations generally had to seek them in the slender archeological collections of museums of natural history. Somehow, ancient Central American objects had been apprehended as having anthropological but not aesthetic significance.

The world has belatedly come to recognize that Central American artists of centuries past were skilled, imaginative, and highly sophisticated in their work, and that the works themselves reflect a series of highly developed cultures. A carved jadeite Olmec mask from Tabasco, Mexico, bears little resemblance to a Chinese butterfly of nephrite from Peking, but each in its own right may be an object of beauty done with exquisite taste and considerable lapidary skill. Part of the reason for the West's late-blooming awareness of and interest in the stone carvings from Central America was that they were unlike anything seen before by Europeans and arose from totally unknown cultures. Jade was not influential in stimulating the "discovery" of America,

and yet the wave of new conquerors met it constantly in worked form.

The Spaniards, during the period of their conquest of Central and South America, sent quantities of gold, jade, and emerald artifacts back to their homeland. Most of the gold objects were melted down for the precious metal itself, to produce coinage or new jewelry. Splendid mosaics, emeralds, and jade carvings were disassembled, recut, and reprocessed into new art objects by European craftsmen; some were even converted for medicinal use. On the whole very little survived in its original form. Consequently, since the Spaniards did not resort to archeological digging, once the readily available supply of objects was exhausted and the cultures themselves were destroyed, knowledge of the art and even of the sources of raw jade was lost.

Not until the early 1900s did serious archeological investigation of these extinct civilizations begin. Now, at an accelerated rate, archeological understanding of Central American civilization and its cultures is growing; and keeping pace with it is a rapid increase in public interest. Nonetheless, the exploratory work is still in its infancy. Only a rough sketch, fairly firm in its outlines, of pre-Columbian history has been developed on an extensive underpinning of solid fact. Obviously, great centers of Mesoamerican civilization, with complex and advanced local cultures, have come and gone through thousands of years. They have left a sparse written record but a wealth of pottery, carved stone, and other artifacts—as well as the ruins of monumental building projects rivaling the finest in the rest of the world.

The Olmecs

The story of jade in the New World probably began when successive waves of Asiatic migrants made their way over the land bridge then existing across the Bering Strait and fanned out eastward and southward into the Western Hemisphere, finally reaching the hospitable lands of Central America, South America, and the Caribbean islands. This may have occurred by 25000 B.C., or even much earlier. By about 5000 B.C., the earliest beginnings of agriculture began to appear among these food-gathering and hunting people. About 1300 B.C., without any signs of gradual development, a highly civilized race of unknown name and language suddenly appeared along the coast of the Gulf of Mexico. Archeologists call these people Olmecs. Their mysterious, influential culture apparently prospered from the time of Pharoah Ramses II of Egypt to the Golden Age of Greece—that is, from approximately 1300 B.C. to 500 B.C. Its influence spread and was felt by all succeeding, better-known cultures of the entire Mesoamerican region over the next 2,000 years. The Olmecs built the first large religious centers, transmitted their worship of the jaguar gods to others, and introduced the earliest calendar and the rudiments of a written language. They also knew and used jade.

The widespread Mesoamerican reverence for jade is constantly reconfirmed with each new major archeological excavation in the region. Early writers mention that, at the death of a dignitary, the corpse was normally dressed richly in finery, feathers, and gold, and a green stone carving was placed on the corpse's tongue. For example, in 1957, Miguel Covarrubias described the contents of a royal burial chamber, dating from the seventh century A.D., in the Temple of Inscriptions (a pyramid tomb) at Palenque in northern Chiapas, Mexico: a personage in the tomb was

> covered with objects of jade which gleamed in brilliant green on the layer of red cinnabar with which the corpse had been painted. On his head he wore a band garnished with large jade spangles. The locks of his hair were held in place by jade tubes, his face was covered by a magnificent mask of jade mosaic with eyes of shell and obsidian, and on his ears he wore a pair of jade earplugs incised with glyphs. His shoulders were covered with a great collar of rows of tubular jade beads, and around his neck there was a precious necklace of beads in the form of calabashes alternating with jade blossoms. His wrists were bound with long strings of jade beads forming cuffs, and on each finger he wore a jade ring, nine of them plain, one carved with the most exquisite delicacy in the shape of a little crouching man. He held a great jade ball in one hand, a square die of jade in the other. There was a fine jade buckle or loincloth ornament, and by his feet was a jade statuette of the Sun God (Covarrubias 1957).

A more typical find was uncovered in 1900–1901 behind the Cathedral in Mexico City. It contained jadeite tablets and approximately 2,000 jadeite beads.

Such jade burial pieces and other miscellaneous jade objects are not limited to Mexico; they have been found in great numbers in a geographic area extending from Mexico to Costa Rica, and more rarely, they appear in the Greater Antilles, Venezuela, Colombia, Panama, and even Peru. The style of carving often helps identify some of the objects as having come from faraway places—like the Olmec and Mayan jades found in Costa Rica. The broad geographical and temporal distributions of miniature axe gods and related objects strongly suggest that these objects were influenced but not directly descended from Olmec culture and may have roots in a tradition even more ancient than the Olmec that once covered most of Middle America.

At Tlatilco, Zacatenco, Ticoman, Gualipita, and El Arbollito in Mexico and at Finca Arizona and Kaminaljuyu in Guatemala, some of the earliest jade objects have been found. Carbon dating at Tlatilco established carving dates close to 1500 B.C., and the art of the area shows decided Olmec influence. Certainly, the Olmecs gave sculptural forms and carving techniques a strong stimulus. They are especially noted for preparing large, fine figures and masks of jade, but they also made innumerable carvings of small boats, stingray pendants, celts, earplugs, bangles, concave plaques, large disks, and necklace beads in flower and animal shapes.

From the Olmec ruins at La Venta in Tabasco, Mexico—a primary Olmec center (from about 1000 B.C. to 600 B.C.) marked by a clay pyramid 103 feet that the craft was imported full-blown by the Olmecs or that developmental artifacts are exceedingly rare.

Some of the earliest Olmec burials contain no jade at all, but a later site in Olmec territory at Cerro de las Mesas on the Gulf of Mexico in the State of Veracruz sheltered a treasure trove of 782 jade objects, many of which were heirlooms from earlier cultures. The theory is that jade was so greatly revered and treasured that it was handed down from generation to generation and therefore frequently escaped burial. Olmec civilization may have disappeared before the birth of Christ, but its influence and the enthusiasm for jade it inculcated were to persist until the conquest.

The Mayans

About 300 B.C., at the time of the Olmec decline, the Mayan culture, occupying the Yucatan Peninsula, gradually began to develop under certain elements of Olmec influence into a high civilization with its own distinctive style. The Mayan culture lasted almost 1,000 years, until overcome by invading Toltecs from the west; the Toltecs' powerful militaristic civilization, in turn, lasted only 300 years.

The Yucatan cultures developed an advanced writing system and were aware of complex mathematical ideas including the use of zero. They had a sophisticated calendar, a unique and recognizable artistic style, and a distinctive architecture—and they, too, revered jade.

The peak of Mayan jade carving skill was reached in a period between A.D. 600 and A.D. 900, during which time they produced enormous numbers of ornaments. They seldom carved masks or figures in the round, as the Olmecs had done, but turned out quantities of well-made beads, tubes, pendants, and plaques carved in high relief. Plaques several inches across often showed a central human figure, either alone or talking to others, surrounded by a series of interesting curvilinear designs. At the famous archeological site of Chichén Itzá in Yucatan the Mayans' sacred cenote, or sacrificial well, has yielded numerous jade pieces. Under the great pyramid temple of Kulkulcán, the plumed serpent god, was found a life-size jaguar carving with seventy-two polished jade disks attached. Not only did the jaguar gods come to the Mayans from the Olmecs but, strangely, so did the practice of using decorative jade insets in the teeth.

Ceremonial blade (4½ inches) surmounted by a squatting figure with a bucket-shaped hat. The blade is one of the pieces carved in the best-quality Central American jadeite ever found. It is Olmec in style and was found in Costa Rica.

tall and famous for four colossal stone heads that were found there—several hundred jade axe forms and statuettes were recovered. The superb rendition of jade figures and jaguar gods worshiped by the Olmecs is strong evidence that the Olmec tradition in jade sprang from much earlier roots. Strangely, even the most ancient Olmec carvings show fully developed carving techniques; no crude carvings appear at the deepest explored levels, implying either

The Aztecs

With the decline of the Mayans, as hastened by the Toltecs, and the subsequent destruction of Tula (stronghold of the Toltecs) by nomadic Chichimecs, a new group began to ascend to power about A.D. 1300. The accumulation of small city-states that remained after the collapse of the Toltecs served as the base of the Aztec civilization. A mere 200 years later, the Spaniards arrived.

It has been well documented that, following the Spaniards' Good Friday landing in 1519, Aztec messengers from the court of Emperor Montezuma II offered Hernando Cortez the first gifts of gold and of jade, which they considered vastly more precious than gold. To the natives of Mesoamerica, the mystical properties of jade—such as the Mayan belief that it would buy food in the next life—and its general connotation of rank and privilege were the source of its value. The most common religious offerings of the Aztecs were bags of rubber, quetzal feathers, human lives, and beads of jade.

Evidently, the only way the Spaniards could account for jade reverence was to attribute to it certain healing powers. To do so was reasonable since much of the established medicinal practice of the day was mystical. Many students of the subject have suggested that the establishment in Europe of this new appreciation of jade (developed through contact with Mesoamerica) encouraged the acceptance and flow of Chinese jade into Europe as the supply from the New World dried up.

The jade wonders of the Aztecs constitute the closing chapter in the tradition of jade artifacts in Mesoamerica. The Aztecs used the material for personal adornment, for sacrifices, for funerary pieces, for decorating idols, and for fancy fastenings for their codices or books. They also made jade masks, pendants, and plaques, as the cultures before them had done for 3,000 years or more. The drastic interruption of these inherited cultural practices by the Spanish conquest, however, brought the jade story to an abrupt end in this part of the world.

Mysteries of Mesoamerican Jade

Several unanswered or poorly answered puzzles have plagued efforts to unravel the story of Central American jade. One that had enormous historical importance and that originally aroused much controversy related to the origin of Mesoamerican jade and of the skills needed to work it. Based on the style of certain jade pieces, the argument was made that commerce at one time existed between Mesoamerica and China. After all, the great jade carvers of the Chou Dynasty were at their peak at a time that overlapped by several centuries the period of Olmec ascendancy. Moreover, Olmec face carvings and masks are decidedly Mongoloid in aspect, and stylistically—if not in carving technique—other similarities are recognizable between Olmec and Chinese carvings. Both cultures rubbed their carvings with red cinnabar, both used jade for burial, commonly placing a piece on the tongue of a corpse, and both had a high reverence for jade.

Ultimately, however, the supposition of a jade trade between the two cultures was exploded by the discovery that Mesoamerican jadeite is a substance quite different from the nephrite used by the Chinese of the Chou Dynasty. Not a single jade artifact mineralogically similar to the jade used in China has ever been found in Mesoamerica. Circumstantial evidence of the nonconnection can be seen in the fact that New World carvers never developed metal tools as the Chinese did. If Chinese jade culture and skills had been imported to Central America, the tools would have come, too. But the most sophisticated Mesoamerican stone carvings were cut, drilled, and polished using volcanic glass abrasives, water, and bamboo, wood, or bone spindles and rubbing tools. Major cutting was done by means of vegetable-fiber strings, water, and abrasives.

Other problems involve the conception of jade itself in the Mesoamerican cultures. The earliest Spanish invaders referred to all green stones as emeralds, not yet being very familiar with the differences between Colombian emerald loot extracted by Pizarro from the Incas of Peru and jade of Central America. Friar Bernardino de Sahagun, in his great work on Aztec culture written between A.D. 1558 and 1569—*Historia General de las Cosas de Nueva España*—also referred to all such stones as emerald, although some were obviously jade. As late as *Compedio del Arte de la Lengua Mexicana*, written by Horatio Carochi in 1645, green gemstones were still being called emerald indiscriminately. These emerald references, however, suggest that the Spaniards were encountering real emerald and also some very select emeraldlike jade in much larger quantities than are known to exist today. Other references in various documents to the ability of "emeralds" to attract moisture suggest a certain confusion with turquoise. Jade (and emerald, too) does not absorb water, but turquoise does. Like jade, turquoise was commonly used by Mesoamerican artisans, but of all the carved minerals found as artifacts in this part of the world—including jade, turquoise, rock crystal, serpentine, amber, onyx, jasper, agate, obsidian, opal, moonstone, and amethyst—jade is the one used most commonly and to greatest aesthetic effect.

Although confusion may have existed as to the name itself, the carvers knew the difference in their materials. The Aztecs have even left an entire hierarchy of names for jade, pointing up their close acquaintance with its characteristics. *Quetzalitzli*, the finest quality, emeraldlike, blue-green jade, was named after the color of the green feathers of the sacred quetzal bird; the term may actually have been reserved for emeralds because *quetzal-chalchihuitl* described another kind of stone that was deep green, translucent, and had no discoloring spots or streaks—such as that used in the very best jade objects found in Olmec country and in Costa Rica. *Chalchihuitl* referred to jade in colors of common green and white, lighter green, green mixed with yellow and white, and other combinations. *Iztacchalchihuitl* was the appellation for white jade with or without colored veins running through it. *Tlilayotic* referred to black or blackish green (like a dark-colored gourd) and was probably applied to what is now called chloromelanite jade. The dark shades generally seem to have been used exclusively for ceremonial tools. *Xiutomolli* was the name given to green or blue-green bonelike jade, which is recognized today as the feldspar mineral amazonite—not jade at all.

Obviously, some confusion with the names will always persist because jade represented a complex of cultural ideas to the ancient Mesoamericans rather than a chemically unique mineralogical substance. Our classification of jadeite and nephrite in terms of chemical specifics would certainly have seemed as strange to them as their system does to us.

One of the greatest puzzles facing archeologists and geologists has been the question of where all the raw Mesoamerican jade came from. The evidence gathered so far indicates that almost all of the raw material was mined in a relatively restricted region of Guatemala. Present-day geologists believe that the jade peculiar to Mesoamerica will only be found in association with certain kinds of serpentine rocks, such as those known in the Sierra de las Minas, the Sierra de Chuacus, and the western shore of Lake Izabal in Guatemala.

After the Spaniards had eradicated local govern-

Two alligator heads hang from a circle pendant carved from some of the finest Central American jadeite. The pendant measures 2½ inches and was found in Costa Rica.

ments and cultures and jade had consequently lost its cultural niche, the native peoples eventually forgot the locations of jade deposits. In the 1950s, however, jade was rediscovered (as predicted) in the valley of the Motagua River near Manzanal, Guatemala; pieces of raw jade and workshop jade from tombs near the Motagua Valley indicate that the area was indeed a jade-working center in pre-Columbian times and a dispersal point for worked objects. For example, a 200-pound mass of jadeite was found at Kaminaljuyu in Guatemala, along with figurines, earplugs, beads, and disks. Another mass, weighing over 100 pounds, was found in El Progresso Province. Both pieces are now on display in the Museum of Archeology in Guatemala City.

No important deposits of jade have ever been found in Mexico. Neither have any traces been found of the beautiful, blue-green, emeraldlike jade that appears in the finest Olmec carvings or in the superb jades preserved in the National Museum in

An exquisitely balanced 5-inch bird celt, found at Las Mercedes, Costa Rica. It is carved in the rare blue-green translucent jadeite of the quality used by the Olmecs, whose Central American source of this jadeite has not yet been rediscovered.

Costa Rica. These ancient Costa Rican carvings superficially resemble Olmec pieces, but they are distinguished by the superb quality of the jade and by the local, sometimes extreme variation in style. The axe-god carvings, the bird celts with their exaggerated beaks, the curly-tailed animals with their exaggerated tails, the frogs, the alligators, and the bats represent Mesoamerican jade culture at its best. And yet the source of this superior-quality jade has not been discovered; geologists only know that it almost certainly did not come from Costa Rica. Searches of the Santa Elena Peninsula (to the north of Nicoya on the Pacific coast), for example, have established that the serpentines there contain no jade.

Despite all the unresolved problems, our knowledge of the Mesoamerican jade cultures and of the sources of jade is likely to develop at a rapid pace, enabling us to learn much more about these civilizations and their artifacts.

EIGHT

NEW ZEALAND JADE

Early New Zealand

The first Polynesians are thought to have arrived in New Zealand from other islands in the Southwest Pacific; the Moahunters, as one group of these Polynesians has been named by anthropologists, had established their nomadic, moa bird-hunting culture on the South Island by A.D. 950. The Moahunters used the stone of their new homeland—including jade, beginning at a very early period—for making weapons and tools.

In the mid-1300s (A.D.), the New Zealand population experienced a sudden upswing in migration of a new group, the Maori, from Polynesia. Maori legend tells of a great migration in enormous canoes capable of holding 70 to 100 people. The newly arriving Maori brought two very significant treasures with them: previous knowledge of jade; and the *kumara (Ipomea batatas)*, a species of sweet potato. Their previous knowledge of jade suggests that some reverse migration to Polynesia by early New Zealand settlers may have occurred, and that these people may have brought back news of the strange land and its valuable green stone resource. The kumara potato was grown under ideal conditions in the north, gradually encouraging the Maori society to abandon its nomadic ways and develop the stability necessary for a high culture.

South of present-day Christchurch, in the colder part of New Zealand, the nomadic hunter culture persisted. Here jade was found and jade-working was developed to supply tools and weapons for local use and for trade with the north to acquire food and textiles. Evidently, jade trading took place not only between North Island and South Island but also between both parts of New Zealand and the people of the Chatham Islands, Raratonga, and Tasmania. In 1970, the main Otago source of the jade used in this early trade was found in the Dart Valley at the head of Lake Wakatipu in Mount Aspiring National Park.

The development of a jade culture by the Maori followed much the same pattern as it did elsewhere. Raw material was fashioned into objects of religious significance, into tools, into weapons, into currency units, and ultimately into objects of art. Unlike the Chinese and the Europeans, the Maori did not assign to jade any magical healing powers. Nevertheless, it was very highly regarded and served as a frequent metaphor in describing the finest human qualities. One of their most significant expressions, ''Let us raise a *tatu pounamu* [jade door],'' was a way of agreeing to make peace or to close the door on war. Unfortunately, many tribal conflicts probably originated over raids for jade, inasmuch as it was frequently included in the booty of local wars.

This ceremonial adze with a typically ornate carved wood handle and highly polished nephrite blade—both too fine to be put to work—once belonged to the Maori chief of the Ngapuhi tribe of New Zealand.

Maori Greenstone

All New Zealand jade is nephrite. Locally it has always borne the name *greenstone* rather than *jade,* but the term *greenstone* is also applied now and then to bowenite, the exceptionally compact and often quite translucent variety of serpentine. A fine deposit of semitransparent to transparent, olive to bluish green bowenite was discovered in Otago at Anita Bay on Milford Sound. Its resemblance to jade was inescapable, so the natives called it greenstone, too, while recognizing its unsuitability as a material for tools and weapons because it could not hold a sharp edge as nephrite does.

The Maori word for New Zealand greenstone is *pounamu.* The word *pou* means "stone" and *namu* is an old Tahitian word for "green." Maori folklore is filled with stories about its origins and discovery, many of which are so fanciful that they defy correlation to fact; the exception is that most of the legends have the jade being recovered from underwater. Much of it has come from stream gravels along the Hokitica, Arahura, and Taramakau rivers. Nephrite sources in the headwaters of the Arahura River are now worked in summer, and the stone is transported by helicopter. The lower tributary rivers and creeks are closely inspected for jade after each flood.

Jade Colors

Although New Zealand jade is noted for its dark green color and partial translucence, individual specimens vary considerably in their characteristics. Accordingly, several descriptive names came early into common usage. Since the Maori had no written language, their history and legends became progressively confused as they were transmitted from generation to generation. The lack of written language also affected jade definitions. Names exist for the various patterns and colors of greenstone, but the meanings these had for different tribes are by no means consistent.

Most of the jade found in New Zealand is intensely dark green to grass green, and the material usually contains numerous impurities in the form of small black flecks. The natives call jade of this color range *kawakawa;* a splendid example of this type, a thin but large slab sliced from an enormous boulder of New Zealand nephrite, is on exhibit in the Gem Hall of the Smithsonian Institution. *Kahurangi* ("highly prized") is a much more translucent variety, which is a light apple or lettuce green and free from dark spots; the Maori used it for making important ceremonial objects. Off-white or gray-green jade, called *inanga,* was the most admired of all and thus was considered best for carving into weapons used as symbols of rank. In recognition of the fact that bowenite was somehow different, it was given the special name *tangiwai* and was reserved for making ornaments and ceremonial objects that did not have to take the working abuse expected of tougher greenstones.

Other, lesser used terms for color varieties also existed. *Auhunga* describes a pale green nephrite intermediate between *inanga* and *kawakawa. Kahotae* is green jade streaked or marked with white. *Raukaraka* is green jade streaked with olive green or with yellow-green. *Totoweka* is the common *kawakawa* variety with reddish spots. Undoubtedly, other names were used to describe types of brown, reddish brown, yellowish brown, and yellow jade that are known among New Zealand nephrite samples. Finally, poor-quality or otherwise undesirable jade was given the special name *tuapaka* or *tutae kiori.*

Maori Artifacts

Assuming that the Maori arrived before A.D. 800, an interval of about 1,000 years elapsed before the first Europeans landed and began to influence the indigenous culture in the late 1700s. This millenium provided sufficient time for the Maori to build up a sizable stock of imperishable jade artifacts, even though each piece was produced with crude implements by agonizingly monotonous hand labor. It was a labor of necessity and love, as the products show.

Maori artifacts are of three types: tools, weapons, and ornaments. Some tools and weapons, however, served also as personal and ceremonial ornaments, and some ornaments and weapons assumed mystical and symbolic significance.

The most important tools of jade were chisels and adzes. Chisels were long and slender enough to be hand-held so that the blunt end could be tapped with a wood mallet to drive the flat, sharpened blade into the wood being cut or carved. Since these were such valuable tools, the habit developed of suspending the chisel from the owner's ear by means of a cord that was also passed through a hole drilled in the chisel. Eventually, this led to development of long, slender, flattened, pencillike, pendant ear ornaments. Jade adzes were used as true adzes and not as axes. A sharp-edged stone was fastened to a wood handle and used for general carpentry and for felling trees. Some of the best jade was reserved for making ceremonial adzes. Although no carving was done on the adze head itself, the wood handle often bore elaborate, deeply cut, uniquely ornate carvings. By contrast, the tools themselves were simple in contour. Adzes and chisels were the primary jade tools, but many others—such as flax scrapers, drill

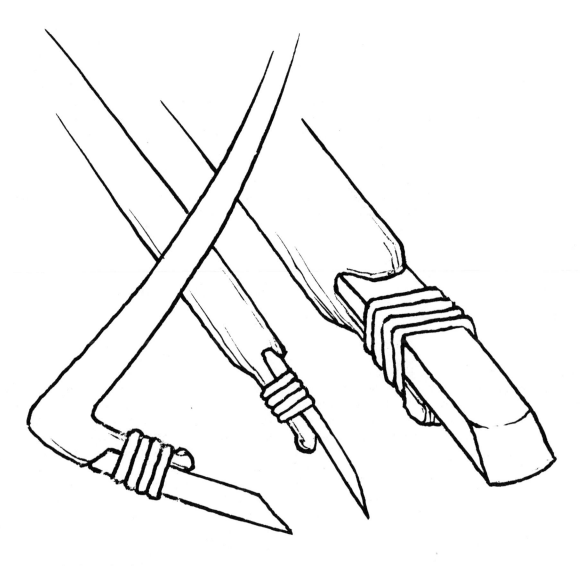

Maori method for fastening jade work tools to wood shafts.

points, fish hook barbs, and even needles—were produced. Among the more unusual items were jade leg rings used in controlling and domesticating the kaka, a native parrot.

Chief among weapons was the greenstone *mere,* which was not only the Maori warrior's most prized weapon but his most prized possession. Hours, days, even years were spent working over it to bring up the polish. The *mere,* also known as a *patu pounamu* (''striking greenstone'') or a *tipi pounamu* (''thrusting greenstone''), is a flattened, rounded, and tapered piece of jade that resembles a short oar, measuring approximately 15 inches long by 5 inches wide (at its widest) by 1 inch thick (at its thickest). The *mere*'s edge is tapered almost to knife sharp-

ness, although the weapon thickens rapidly away from the edge. Weighing approximately 5 to 7 pounds, the *mere* typically has a hole drilled through the butt end to allow insertion of a wrist cord; in use, the cord was tied or looped around the warrior's wrist. In hand-to-hand fighting, the weapon was rather gruesomely effective at crushing, disemboweling, and decapitating enemies. Like the adze, the *mere* was ground flat and smooth and never ornamented with surface carving. It was the only weapon ever made of jade; other materials, such as bone, were also used for the purpose—and bowenite might be enlisted for *meres* intended only for ceremonial purposes.

As with other jade cultures, the Maori are best

known not for their tools or weapons but for their ornaments and works of art. These are limited in design, motif, and imagination but are extremely attractive in their simplicity. No jade earplugs, beads, bracelets, or finger rings were produced—only pendant ornaments of one kind or another. Unlike the natives' unadorned jade tools, Maori pendants and amulets were usually carved elaborately and deeply, as were their distinctive wooden artifacts. Some of these pendants measured as much as 15 inches long, and all were designed to be worn dangling from the earlobe or around the neck. *Kuru* were pencil-shaped pendants; *kurupapu* were long but flattened; and *kapeu* were flat with curved ends, rather like miniature hockey sticks. Of course, many intermediate designs were also possible.

Best known and most coveted of all the pendant ornaments was the *hei tiki—hei* meaning "neck pendant," and *tiki* meaning "humanoid" or "human." Typically they were worn suspended on a plaited cord, one end of which formed a loop, and the other of which was tied to a 3-inch piece of bird bone (through a hole in the middle of the bone). The bone, when passed through the loop, made a practical fastening. The *hei tiki* themselves are flat pendants carved into grotesque human forms with large, round eyes and with heads cocked to one side. To heighten the bizarre effect, the round eyes were inset in the early days with pava shell *(Haliotis iris)*. Following the arrival of the Europeans, red sealing wax was a common substitute for shell.

Such pendants were not idols of gods or talismans in the usual sense; they were representations of human beings, most often ancestors—memorials to all who had worn them in the past. *Hei tiki* were worn by both men and women, and some of the best were so highly treasured (intrinsically and for their ancestor association) that they were passed down through several generations of a family. A measure of the widespread popularity of this form of pendant amulet among the Maori is that twenty-three *hei tiki* were dug up at one site at Murdering Beach near Dunedin. This was originally a native village, burnt by rapacious European seal hunters in 1817.

The Maori also made other kinds of amulets, whose meanings are now obscure but whose forms are easily traceable to objects with which the people were familiar. The *hei matau,* for example, is a stylized Maori fishhook that probably evolved from a beginning as a precious fishhook hung around the neck for safe keeping. Zoomorphic amulets include the *pekapeka* (a bat) and the *marakihau* (a sea monster), which in all its known carvings looks like some

kind of bird-headed beast. The *koropepe,* with its spiral form, appears to represent some sort of snake. No land snakes exist in New Zealand, however, so it either records a design carried by the Polynesians from their home islands to the new land or depicts a sea snake or eel (though the degree of coiling presented in the carvings is not natural to the eel).

European Influence

The jade art forms the Maori were developing in their weapons, tools, and ornaments were rudely interrupted through appearance of the European explorer on the scene. Captain James Cook, the first European to give extensive accounts of New Zealand, landed in the late 1700s; from his voyage narratives, word began to filter back to Europe about the remarkable race of people inhabiting New Zealand and about their jade. On another of Cook's voyages, in 1771, John Hawkesworth of *Gentleman's Magazine* made note of the native uses for a "green talc-like stone which is not only hard but tough." In 1778, J. R. Forester, who accompanied Captain Cook to New Zealand, made the first recorded mention of New Zealand jade, although he misspelled it as *jadde.*

Almost from the first, Maori jade objects (particularly the *hei tiki*) were zealously sought by collectors. A brisk trade rapidly developed, and soon all available jade tools, weapons, and ornaments had been drained off to Europe. The demand for them was so great that the Maori developed an industry to manufacture amulets for the trade, and as a result the objects lost their original significance. The introduction of iron tools and weapons and the ultimate subjugation of the people completed the disruption of the jade culture, ending most of the interest of native artisans in producing jade objects.

Nevertheless, New Zealand jade deposits represent a potential supply for the jade-hungry world. Considerable modern prospecting uncovered new supplies and encouraged a revival of jade-cutting in Australia and New Zealand. Some of the artistry displayed in new carvings cleverly imitates and adapts old Maori designs, but the emphasis today is largely European. New Zealand jade no longer focuses on tools, weapons, and ancestor amulets but on modern ornamentation. In an attempt to support this local industry, the government has outlawed the export of rough or unworked jade from New Zealand.

Other Jade in Oceania

Not surprisingly, when a survey is made of the occurrence of jade artifacts elsewhere in Oceania, it appears that the Maori might have had knowledge of jade before they came to New Zealand. Ancient jade tools have been found widely scattered in such places as the Loyalty Islands and even Tasmania. A fine nephrite adze measuring about 4½ inches in length has been recovered from the gravels of Tasmania's north coast.

Interestingly enough, most jades such as these are traceable not to New Zealand but to the small island of Ouen, off the southeast point of New Caledonia, where an ancient nephrite quarry that shows signs of extensive work has been discovered. On New Caledonia itself jade objects are plentiful. In 1886, Dr. A. B. Meyer described some of the peculiar weapons from the island. There are, he said, "large oval hatchets, called *nbouets,* with which the enemies were slaughtered and cut to pieces." One of these hatchets, admittedly a large one, was 1 foot in blade diameter and was mounted on an 18-inch wood handle.

Another major cache of jade artifacts in the vast Southwest Pacific region has been uncovered in New Guinea. The Dresden Museum contains about 300 stone tools from New Guinea, many of which are reported to be jadeite, nephrite, and chloromelanite. This is not unexpected because jade deposits, including chloromelanite and worked and unworked nephrite, have been found scattered throughout New Guinea. In the Cyclops Mountains in particular, the natives made frequent use of nephrite for hatchets and other implements. Even jade rings up to 4 inches in diameter, which were obviously intended for ceremonial purposes, have been discovered on this large island.

Jade deposits have also been found on Celebes in Indonesia, and undoubtedly others will be found elsewhere.

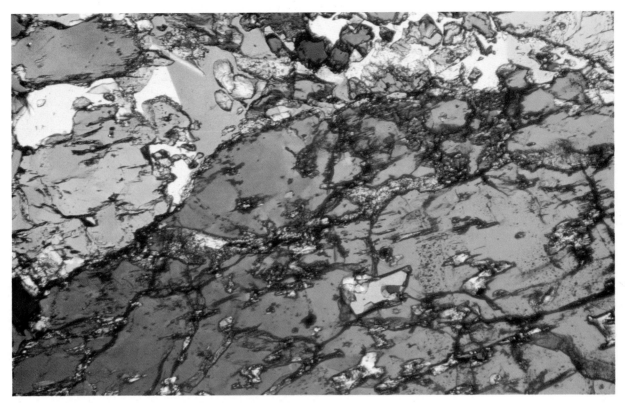

Rock thin section of Guatemalan jadeite, shown under polarized light. Photo courtesy of the Smithsonian Institution, Washington, D.C.

Rock thin section of Taiwan nephrite, shown under polarized light. Photo courtesy of the Smithsonian Institution, Washington, D.C.

Rock thin section of Burmese jadeite, shown under polarized light. Photo courtesy of the Smithsonian Institution, Washington, D.C.

A rock thin section of Burmese jadeite, shown under polarized light. Photo courtesy of the Smithsonian Institution, Washington, D.C.

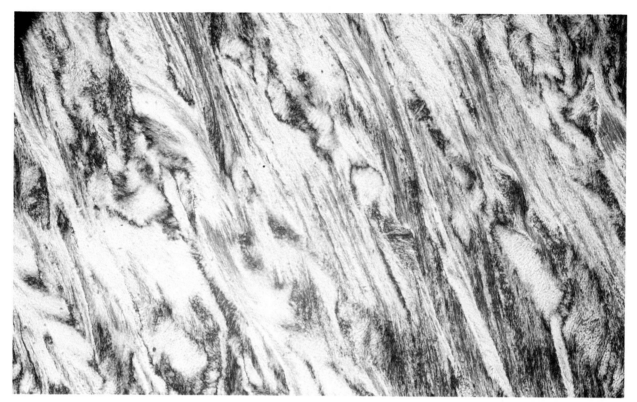

Rock thin section of nephrite obtained near Gratz, Austria; shown under polarized light. Photo courtesy of the Smithsonian Institution, Washington, D.C.

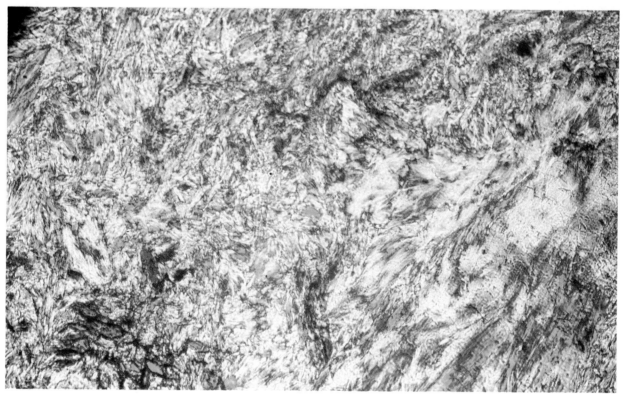

Rock thin section of nephrite from the Lake Baikal area, U.S.S.R. Shown under polarized light. Photo courtesy of the Smithsonian Institution, Washington, D.C.

Rock thin section of Japanese jadeite, shown under polarized light. Photo courtesy of
the Smithsonian Institution, Washington, D.C.

Archaic human figure of nephrite, probably dating
from the Han Dynasty in China. Photograph by
Dane Penland. Smithsonian Institution Collection.

Nephrite cicada, a grave piece placed on the tongue of
the corpse, probably dating from the Han Dynasty in
China. Photograph by Dane Penland. Smithsonian
Institution Collection.

Delicate, translucent jadeite bowls with matching lids, dating from the Ch'ing Dynasty. The bowls are approximately 4½ inches in diameter. Photograph by Dane Penland. Smithsonian Institution Collection.

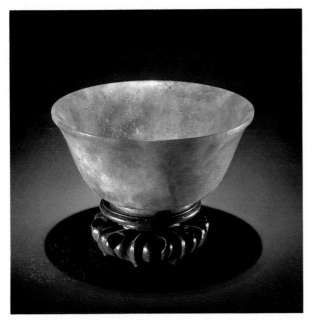

A large Revere-style bowl of fine green Burmese jadeite, carved during the Ch'ing Dynasty. Bowl diameter is approximately 12 inches. Photograph by Dane Penland. Smithsonian Institution Collection.

A pair of nephrite altar lanterns, each approximately 18 inches tall. Carved during the Ch'ing Dynasty, the globes are thin enough to be translucent but are also carved in open work to transmit light. Photograph by Dane Penland. Smithsonian Institution Collection.

A large, shallow, thin-walled translucent nephrite bowl, carved in the chrysanthemum pattern popular in the Ch'ing Dynasty. The bowl is approximately 12 inches in diameter, and its wall is about 1/16 inch thick. Photograph by Dane Penland. Smithsonian Institution Collection.

An ancient Chinese form, the ts'ung represents things of the earth. This 1⅞- × 2¼-inch ts'ung from Eastern Chou Dynasty times is classically simple and unadorned. Photograph by Harold and Erica Van Pelt. Crystalite Collection.

A Ch'ing Dynasty carving in nephrite depicting citrus medica—a part of the plant often called Buddha's fingers. Because of its connection with Buddha, the form has become a symbol of good fortune. Photograph by Harold and Erica Van Pelt.

A pair of tou standing approximately 13 inches tall. These Ch'ing Dynasty green nephrite carvings have inlays of white nephrite. Photo courtesy of the Smithsonian Institution, Washington, D.C.

Modern Chinese carving of a Kuan Yin figure of high-quality, natural-color Burmese jadeite (height approximately 9 inches). The green rabbit is a symbol of long life. Photograph by Dane Penland. Smithsonian Institution Collection.

Large, modern Chinese carving, approximately 22 inches tall. This vase, of five-colored, very high quality Burmese jadeite, was carved in the Ch'ien Lung style and has a copy of the Ch'ien Lung seal on the bottom. Photograph by Dane Penland. Smithsonian Institution Collection.

A typical carved Chinese mountain from the eighteenth century. The multicolored nephrite piece measures 6¾ × 4 inches and depicts a Taoist wise man strolling in an idyllic Chinese landscape. Photograph by Harold and Erica Van Pelt. Crystalite Collection.

Modern Chinese serpentine carving of two figures. Serpentine of this quality is the commonest jade substitute. Photograph by Lee Boltin. Smithsonian Institution Collection.

Burmese jadeite cabochons and bracelet of bright and unusual natural colors. Photograph by Lee Boltin. Smithsonian Institution Collection.

A nephrite vase—one of a pair of modern carvings by T. C. Chang—carved in Ch'ien Lung style of Alaskan nephrite found by George Van Hagen near Jade Mountain, Alaska. Photographed by Lee Boltin. Lizzadro Museum Collection.

Two pieces, from a Russian desk set, carved of high-quality translucent Russian nephrite. Photo courtesy of the Smithsonian Institution, Washington, D.C.

Cabochons of Madagascar amazonstone, a somewhat reasonable jade substitute in terms of color and hardness. Photo courtesy of the Smithsonian Institution, Washington, D.C.

A bowl carved of amazonstone, a look-alike jade substitute, from the Amelia Court House in Virginia. Photo courtesy of the Smithsonian Institution, Washington, D.C.

Pair of jadeite bowls showing the occurrence of bright green blotches in a mass of whitish Burmese jade. Photograph by Lee Boltin. Smithsonian Institution Collection.

Pair of staff-bearing figures from Costa Rica, made of translucent blue-green jadeite. The staffs have serpent heads and small birds at the top. Photograph by Lee Boltin.

Narrow axe-god of translucent blue-green jadeite. Photograph by Lee Boltin.

Human figurine of translucent jadeite from Costa Rica. This 4½-inch piece was drilled at the eyes and at the cord-sawed openings so that it could be worn as a pendant. Photograph by Lee Boltin. American Museum of Natural History Collection.

Aztec jewelry pendant in jadeite and gold, dating from A.D. 1450 to 1520. Photograph by Lee Boltin.

Mayan mask, probably of serpentine, from Tikal, Mexico. The mask has inset eyes and teeth, and has holes drilled so that it may be worn as a pendant. Photograph by Lee Boltin.

Winged 6-inch pendant (above) and beaked bird (right), both of jadeite found in Costa Rica. The bird measures 2³/₈ inches. Photograph by Lee Boltin. American Museum of Natural History Collection.

Mayan pendant of the sun god Kinich Ahau. Dating from A.D. 600 to 900, the pendant is 3½ inches tall and is carved of Guatemalan jadeite. Photograph by Lee Boltin. University of Pennsylvania Museum Collection.

An Olmec jadeite mask illustrating typical mongoloid facial appearance, with large Guatemalan jadeite beads. Photograph by Dane Penland. Smithsonian Institution Collection.

A typical Mayan plaque carving of Guatemalan jadeite, showing a seated dignitary. The width is approximately 6 inches. Photograph by Lee Boltin. Peabody Museum Collection.

Seated Olmec jadeite figure, reddened with red cinnabar. Height about 5 inches.
Photograph by Lee Boltin. American Museum of Natural History Collection.

Mayan pendant of the sun god Kinich Ahau. Dating from A.D. 600 to 900, the pendant is 3½ inches tall and is carved of Guatemalan jadeite. Photograph by Lee Boltin. University of Pennsylvania Museum Collection.

An Olmec jadeite mask illustrating typical mongoloid facial appearance, with large Guatemalan jadeite beads. Photograph by Dane Penland. Smithsonian Institution Collection.

A typical Mayan plaque carving of Guatemalan jadeite, showing a seated dignitary. The width is approximately 6 inches. Photograph by Lee Boltin. Peabody Museum Collection.

Seated Olmec jadeite figure, reddened with red cinnabar. Height about 5 inches.
Photograph by Lee Boltin. American Museum of Natural History Collection.

A variety of jade carvings, of both jadeite and nephrite, from Burma, Guatemala, Wyoming, and California. Photograph by Dane Penland. Smithsonian Institution Collection.

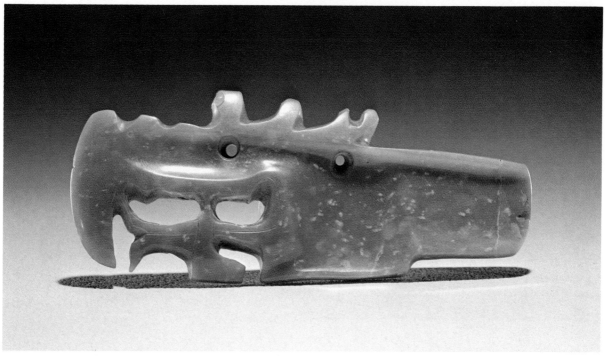

An ancient beaked celt from Costa Rica, carved of some of the best blue-green jadeite found in Mesoamerica. Photograph by Lee Boltin. F. R. Pleasants Collection.

Bow-driven cutting wheel for hand-held grinding and polishing of cabochons, shown in a typical native cutting shop near Ratnapura, Sri Lanka.

A necklace of extraordinary almost-transparent emerald-green jadeite from Burma—the so-called Imperial Jade.

A delicate carving of three figures in rare translucent white nephrite. The figures stand approximately 6 inches tall. Photograph by Dane Penland. Smithsonian Institution Collection.

Typical hei-tiki from New Zealand, carved of the local nephrite and inset with mother-of-pearl eyes. Photograph by Lee Boltin. American Museum of Natural History Collection.

NINE

SOUTH-CENTRAL ASIA, INDIA, RUSSIA, AND JAPAN

South-central Asia

In A.D. 1405, the last remains of Tamerlane—founder of the Timurid Dynasty of south-central Asia—were laid to rest in a deep crypt under an enormous slab of jade at the Gur Emir Mosque of Samarkand (now part of Uzbek in the Soviet Union). Although broken through the middle at some time in the distant past, the slab is still there, measuring 7 feet, 8 inches long and weighing 1,800 pounds. It is of the darkest kind of green jade, well polished, and completely covered with inscriptions. The slab rests on a white marble base and obviously was originally quarried some 600 miles to the east of Samarkand, in the ridge of Raskendaria in Yarkand, the Sinkiang source of Chinese nephrite.

The last of the Timurids was Baber the Tiger, who established the Mogul Empire in India after leading his armies south to capture Delhi in the early 1500s. The empire was finally stabilized by Akbar, Baber's grandson, in the middle to late 1500s. Although Samarkand had been lost even at the time of Baber's initial invasion of Delhi, the Mogul Empire under Akbar encompassed much territory, including Afghanistan, most of northern India, and parts of what is now the Soviet Union.

India

In the process of conquest, the Moguls developed a taste for culture and opulence that has seldom been matched and has helped give India its reputation for fabulous treasures. The reigns of Akbar's son Jahangir and grandson Shah Jahan (who ruled from 1627 to 1658) were marked by wealth, grandeur, and an outpouring of works of art. Shah Jahan expanded the empire to include southern India. It was he, called the "great builder," who ordered construction of the Taj Mahal as a tomb for himself and his wife, Mumtaz Mahal. This monument, visited by hordes of tourists today, is decorated with nephrite floral inlays, among other gemstones.

For centuries, caravans have carried jade and other precious articles from the east to India and

A 3½-inch drinking cup, carved of rich, dark brown nephrite probably during the T'ang Dynasty (A.D. 618 to 906). This particular carving has been pointed out as an example of Western, possibly Persian, influence because it is so unlike the usual Chinese carvings in style and has features common to Western metal sculptures and pottery. Photo courtesy of the San Francisco Center of Asian Art and Culture.

capital were busy cutting and carving jade and developing a unique Mogul style of jade art. It is sometimes presumed that these master cutters, who produced such superbly wrought works, were imported from the lapidary shops of China. If so, they quickly abandoned their Chinese approach to jade or gave birth to a generation of artistically independent carvers.

As can be seen in the great collections of Mogul jades—in the Victoria and Albert Museum in London, for example—the great Indian jade pieces are not at all Chinese in concept. Rather than letting the jade dominate the nature of the carving, these pieces blend the finest material with precious metals and inset precious gems to create elaborately embellished objects. Jade among the Moguls was used as just another precious ornamental stone. A typical creation—for example, an urn, a vase, or a sword hilt—would employ a translucent, light-colored jade that might be lightly carved over most of its surface but whose major features would be floral or arabesque designs made of gems set in gold and inlaid in the jade. Sometimes the jade itself was cut in open fretwork and might even have vividly enameled metal inlays or adjuncts to heighten the colorful, decorative effect.

Not all Indian jade pieces were so heavily decorated. In Shah Jahan's time, a trend emerged toward exquisite, Chinese-style carvings of unembellished jade, designed to take advantage of the stone's translucence. Thin-walled cups, bowls, and other objects attested not only to the skill of the carvers but also to the strength of the jade. Later, under Shah Jahan's son, Emperor Aurangzeb, work tended again toward heavier embellishment. Jade sword and dagger hilts were encrusted with enamels and gems; even jade book covers were produced, with gold hinges and settings of precious gems. The French historian, Francois Bernier, spent twelve years in the emperor's court and reported that, on one occasion, the King of Tibet (who was expecting imminent invasion) sent gifts to the emperor that included a large jade stone. Under Aurangzeb, the empire began to fall apart but the Mogul's love of jade persisted to the end.

The Chinese were undoubtedly aware of Mogul jade art, and some students believe that much of the work seen in Delhi was actually done in China. If so, it was done wholly for export, since none of it appeared in China until the mid-1600s, when pieces began to arrive as tribute to the Chinese emperor. All are agreed that by the eighteenth century the Chinese carvers were copying some of the elements

thence farther west. No deposits of jade were known of old in India, however, so an independent native lore of jade was not developed. Chinese ideas about medicinal uses for the stone, as well as some appreciation of its mystical qualities, were introduced along with the jade. When the Moguls conquered much of the subcontinent, the jade they had learned to love was accessible from deposits in Burma, Tibet, and Eastern Turkestan. Even bowenite, known to the Moguls as *sang i yeshm*, could be recovered from a good deposit in Afghanistan and shipped down the Indus River to Delhi, the capital of the empire.

Although the original Indian civilization was almost as old as that of the Chinese, it concerned itself little with jade until the Mogul invasion from the north in A.D. 1525 brought in supplies of jade and created an interest in working it. By the latter half of the sixteenth century, lapidary shops in Akbar's

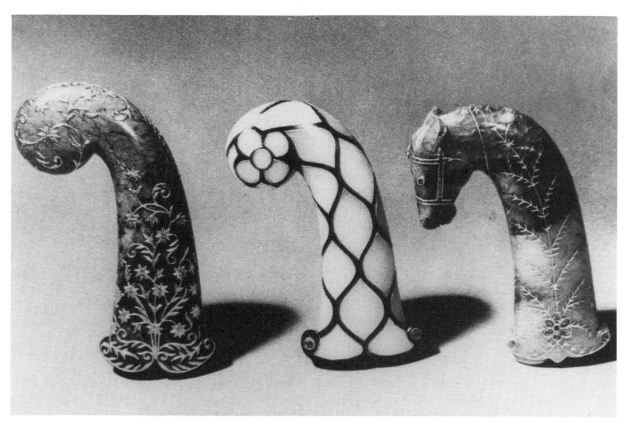

Three seventeenth- and eighteenth-century Mogul-style nephrite dagger handles. Measuring approximately 5 inches, they illustrate the intricate and varied styles commonly used in India to embellish jade. The center handle is carved in dark green nephrite inlaid with white nephrite.

of the Mogul jade style; as a result, it is extremely difficult—if not impossible—to detect the difference between a Mogul original and an eighteenth-century Chinese imitation. Whether originals or imitations, the pieces are few and almost all are superb, so each has become a cherished collector's item.

Russia

About 1850, J. P. Alibert, a French engineer, was mining graphite near Batugol in the Sayan Mountains of Siberia. Nearby, in an outcrop on the banks of the Onut, nephrite lay exposed in considerable quantity. After Alibert's discovery, more was found in other streams in the region. The attention of Europe was thus attracted to this fine, light- to medium-green jade peppered with tiny black flecks. Alibert originally assumed that the black flecks

were graphite, but they have since proved to be chromite. As a monument to the discovery, a man-high 1,156-pound, highly polished boulder of this jade stands in the British Museum of Natural History, signed by Alibert himself.

No one knows how long Siberian nephrite was recognized outside the region before Alibert's time; however, for a number of years previously, it did make its way to China, Korea, Japan, and perhaps elsewhere. The Chinese even gave it the special name of *po ts'ai yu* ("spinach jade").

Prehistoric human beings within the region—and indeed through most of European Russia—knew and used jade, as is attested by an ample supply of jade axeheads and other implements found in prehistoric tombs. The Scythians, an ancient race of Indo-Iranian nomads, established the center of their kingdom (several centuries before the fourth century B.C.) on the north shore of the Black Sea and extended their influence into surrounding territories. Either they or the natives they conquered used jade for tools and ornaments. The Soyots, natives of the western Lake Baikal region, are known to have used jade for hundreds of years for bead necklaces and other ornaments. Russian archeologist A. P. Okladnikov claims that, by 2000 B.C., jade was being used for axes, ornaments, and trade pieces in this region.

The passage of centuries of Russian history eventually brought a return, full circle, to the elaborateness of Tamerlane's tomb. When Czar Alexander II was assassinated in 1881, the royal family began a search for slabs of jade out of which to fashion his sarcophagus. More jade was sought for a large canopy to be built over the tomb of Czar Alexander III, when he died in 1894.

Jade objects of art reached their highest level of sophistication in Russia in the hands of Peter Carl Faberge. In 1884, under Alexander III, he received a court appointment for his family goldsmithy and jeweler's establishment to prepare jeweled objects for the czars. His shops created, among other things, the famous jeweled Easter eggs, which are now exhibited with pride in important museums. Altogether fifty-eight of these eggs were made through the years, and the stone bases of some of them was made wholly or in part of Siberian jade. Because of the jade's excellent cutting characteristics, Faberge's workers found it an excellent medium: tough, capable of taking exquisite detail, and uniform in texture and color. Royal tastes and artistic trends of the time caused his embellished and ornamented stone creations to lean more toward the artistic tradition of the Mogul craftsmen and of the art shops of Rudolph II of the Holy Roman Empire in the seventeenth century than to modern European traditions.

Japan

As has been mentioned, almost no race in eastern Europe, Asia, or Oceania failed to have at least some contact with jade during its prehistory. The Japanese, so close to China and its sources, were no exception. In Idzumo Province, for example, prehistoric sites have been found that are littered with unfinished and broken beads, waste stone materials, and grinding and polishing stones, with some jade included. It is true that the kinds of jade artifacts found in Japan are limited, but jade celts, axes, hammers, and beads have been found. Old celts found loose in the soil were obviously made for hafting with wood handles. Some of the blades had been sharpened and polished on both sides, while others that resemble typical chisels had been ground on only one side of the cutting edge.

The most interesting Japanese tomb artifacts are of a type called *magatama* ("curved bead"), which refers to peculiar comma-shaped beads that measure from ½ to 4 inches long and are drilled at the large end for stringing. Such beads have been recovered from second- and third-century tombs, and oddly enough, they have also been found in fourth- to sixth-century Korean tombs. At Keishu, Korea, for example, one tomb contained no less than fifty *magatama*. In an excavation at Kyongju, once the capital of the Korean kingdom of Silla, archeologists recovered a fancy gold crown dating from the sixth or seventh century A.D. and heavily decorated with *magatama*. Along with the beads, a number of *kudatama*, long cylindrical beads, have also been found. Like *magatama*, most *kudatama* are made of jadeite, although a few are of nephrite. Ancient drawings of *magatama* and *kudatama* show them being worn as personal ornaments in strings around the waist or hanging from the neck to the waist.

The great problem defying solution here is that both types of beads are composed of jadeite and not nephrite. In the second to sixth centuries, nephrite jade might easily have been imported to Japan from Chinese jade-cutting centers near the coast; however, China did not possess or even recognize jadeite until centuries later. All cutting prior to the eighteenth century was being done upon Khotan and Yarkand nephrite.

A possible source for the jadeite might lie in Korea itself. Old records mention an occurrence in northwest Korea of jade that was said to be different from Chinese jade and, therefore, might have been jadeite. Another possible source was uncovered in 1950 when an American geologist, H. S. Yoder, reported an occurrence of jadeite in the bed of the Kotai River in Japan. This was later corroborated by the Japanese Geological Survey, which described the occurrence as similar to those in Burma and California but generally of poor quality and in very limited supply. Some of the grayish to white material contains fairly bright green spots, but these specimens are rare, and only a few cabochons have been cut from Japanese jadeite. The Kotai River jadeite deposit is now preserved as a national treasure, and mining of the rock is prohibited. Perhaps the most incredible fact of all is that, with the wholesale transplants of Chinese culture in every form to Japan, the love of jade and the traditional jade forms never took root there.

TEN

JADE IN EUROPE

Early Europe

Although the Romans traded with India and the Orient, no remnants of Chinese jade or jade objects whatsoever have been discovered in the Roman ruins or among the relics of Etruscan civilization. Some of the Roman references to emeralds could easily have been to jade, but no evidence exists to support the idea.

Very little is known of Greek jade objects. Onomakritos, writing about 500 B.C., does mention a grass-green jasper that may have been jade. When Dr. Heinrich Schliemann, the famous archeologist, was excavating at Kissarlik in Asia Minor in 1879 during his search for ancient Troy, he managed to unearth thirteen nephrite implements. The jade of these implements very strongly resembles Khotan jade. A deposit of jadeite is known on the island of Syros, which from 3000 B.C. to 2000 B.C. was headquarters for much of the trade in the Aegean Sea region. Elsewhere in the Hellenic world, some few celts of jadeite have been found in Crete, and nephrite artifacts have turned up in various parts of Greece.

Significant discoveries of jadeite, nephrite, and chloromelanite implements used by neolithic lake dwellers in Switzerland indicate that Europe, in many scattered places, had prehistoric to ancient contact with and appreciation of jade and its qualities.

Controversies of Source and Name

Two aspects of an earlier controversy surrounding European jades should be mentioned. First, an early conviction arose that jade artifacts being found in Europe must have been made of material imported from the Orient because no source of jade in Europe was known at the time. This argument has since been settled with subsequent discoveries of jade deposits in Germany, Italy, Switzerland, and elsewhere in Europe.

The first reported find was a deposit near Jordansmuhl in Silesia (at the time in Germany, but now part of Poland) by Herman Traube of Breslau (Wroclaw). Later he discovered still another near Reichenstein (Dzierzoniow). In 1889 the famous American gemologist, George Kunz, visited Silesia and found one of the largest nephrite boulders to remain preserved today in its original state. On display at the American Museum of Natural History in New York, this jade weighs 4,710 pounds and looks remarkably like Siberian nephrite. Elsewhere, deposits have been reported from the Harz Mountains of East Germany and Frankenwald forest in West Germany. Ample evidence has now been found that several of these rediscovered deposits were worked by prehistoric cultures.

The second controversy about European jade lies in the confusion of jade names and whether or not early literature references to stone called green jasper and to other green stones were actually references to jade. In 1746 in England, John Hill translated the famous treatise on gemstones written by Theophrastus in 315 B.C. At one point, he noted that the name *prasius* (green jasper) more properly belongs to *lapis nephriticus* (nephrite). In 1880, Jean Pierre Abel Remusat, a French Oriental scholar, supplied evidence for his view that a link existed between the Hebrew *yashpeh* and the green jasper of the Greeks and Romans—one ultimately identifying both with jade.

Undoubtedly, the jade-jasper confusion in early literature will never be completely disentangled, but it is historically safe now (in light of recently uncovered evidence) to suppose that many, if not all, early references to green jasper—as well as many remarks about emeralds—really refer to jade. Therefore, statements like that of Dr. Story-Maskelyne of the British Museum, made in 1880 in response to a query from Dr. Schliemann, must now be taken at a much diminished value. He had said, "The Assyrians and Egyptians, like all other peoples, have valued green stones. Green jasper and amazonstone, and even plasma, were known and appreciated; why not jade also? My answer would be that they could not get it." The chances are that they did know it (and loved it), but the local supply was nonexistent; consequently, the few pieces brought in by trade with Europe and the Orient, directly or indirectly, have been too scattered to leave traces.

To put the loss of such archeological traces into perspective, we need only consider what happened to the Mesoamerican jade objects brought to Europe by the Spaniards within the past 500 years. As mentioned before, Spanish explorers are thought to have first encountered jade along the Yucatan coast in 1518. From that moment on (but starting slowly), a flood of jade objects poured into Europe. But today, relatively little of that flood can be found. Some Mesoamerican pieces reside in museums, but the bulk of the work has disappeared or been distributed to private collections that are seldom publicized.

At any rate, with the advent of American jade on the European scene, an as yet unquenched desire developed for this green stone. Europe did not develop its own jade style, however, nor did it develop (except at Idar-Oberstein, Germany) important stone cutting and polishing centers. The cutting establishments privately supported by wealthy patrons—whenever they carved in jade at all—borrowed heavily from Mogul and Chinese style.

ELEVEN

CUTTING AND CARVING JADE

Because only Chinese jade carving has continued to develop through the centuries up to our own time, it offers the longest uninterrupted picture of how jade carving might have evolved elsewhere if it had been continued. A jade carving tradition was well established in China by the time of the Shang Dynasty (1600 B.C. to 1027 B.C.). Rotary drills and tools were in common use during the western Han Dynasty (206 B.C. to 8 A.D.). The tradition burst into its most ornate period in the 1700s and 1800s. Great quantities of fine carvings, many of extraordinary size, eventually poured out of the studios of Emperor Ch'ien Lung in the middle to late 1700s.

By contrast, the jade art of the Central American lapidaries, although it flowered during the same period, suffered from lack of good carving material, and then died abruptly with the arrival of the Spaniards. In China, even the advent of the communist state, on the heels of the last Manchu emperor and the first republic, did not stop it. For a short period the craft was outlawed, but it quickly returned to favor as a way of attracting foreign currency.

Early Techniques for Carving Jade

Long ago, people discovered they could shape jade fragments for their own purposes and that the arduous work involved was worth doing. The oldest jade artifacts recovered are simple axeheads, knife blades, and wedges—objects of a very practical nature. Early human beings soon learned that jade could (with difficulty) be honed to a fine edge and, unlike other stone tools, would keep its edge under hard use.

What is surprising is the early production of such tools in small or large sizes, so thinly and beautifully carved as to be almost useless for the purposes suggested by their forms. These pieces were ceremonial or token objects that were never intended for hard use but that took advantage of the characteristics of jade to create delicate objects in addition to the more practical tools.

Jade cutting is actually a process of abrasion in

which the jade is rubbed repeatedly with harder material, so that it is slowly worn away until it attains the desired shape. The fragment first needs to be reduced to the appropriate size; a suitable abrasive substance must then be selected and applied to the fragment with considerable energy, using some appropriate tool. Because it is such a durable material, jade has always been difficult to shape. The ancient breaking and chipping techniques commonly used on flint, obsidian, and other materials are totally useless for jade in consequence of the very toughness and resistance to breakage for which it has been so highly prized.

Even with today's much more advanced cutting and carving technology, jade can still be difficult to process. No matter how skilled the cutter, some jades even now present seemingly insoluble problems of undercutting (small surface depressions due to the stone's having spots of variable hardness) or plucking (surface pits left by tiny fragments of stone that were pulled out by the abrasive). Numerous "secret" techniques have been developed by stone cutters in an attempt to solve these problems, since an attack that works with one piece will often fail with another.

In all the history of jade carving, only a few basic developments have emerged to facilitate the process. Technological development has brought about improvements in abrasives and abrasive tools, and the conversion from human- to machine-powered processes. In these days of high technology, instant handicrafts, and assembly-line production of art objects, it is difficult to imagine the degree of hard work required in the past to complete a fine Chinese jade carving. Given the problems an artisan would have encountered in carving even a small object, it is a staggering thought that, during the time of the great Chinese jade patron, Emperor Ch'ien Lung, great numbers of carvings were made, and blocks weighing as much as 7 tons were worked successfully.

Eyewitness accounts of jade working by the early Maori of New Zealand offer some insight into methods that must have been commonly used in all early jade carving cultures. With a large *kuru* (a jade hammer), the miner broke out pieces of jade from the main mass. To assist in dividing large masses properly, grooves were cut in the jade by rubbing it with a quartz-rich mica schist known as *kiripaka*. The quartz grains, with a hardness of 7, readily wore away the nephrite (whose hardness was 6½). These grooves helped to limit later breaking to predetermined directions. The final cutting and polish-

ing were accomplished over long periods of rubbing with a *hoanga* ("hard stone").

The early Maori also stumbled onto the rotary drill, or *pirori*, which they successfully employed for cutting and shaping jade. Unlike those used by other primitive carvers, Maori drills were neither stone-tipped nor hollow; either of these adaptations would have expedited the work well beyond anything possible with the simple rotating stick, sand, and water method they used. Until the mid-1800s, no metal tools were used by the Maori—in contrast with Chinese carving technology, which had adopted metal tools many centuries earlier.

Pre-Columbian carvers in Central America also worked without metal, using bone, wood, reeds, and even cactus needles in their drills. Reportedly, an accidentally broken carving, at Chicago's Field Museum of Natural History, exposed the embedded tip of a bird-bone drill equipped with a bit of abrasive grit. Friar Bernardino de Sahagun, chronicler of Central American culture during the Spanish conquest, described the local work on jades: "They are polished, ground, worked with abrasive sand glued with bat excrement, rubbed with a fine cane, made to shine" (Sahagun, translated 1955). Volcanic sand was the kind used primarily. Depressions were carved by drilling several holes close together and rubbing the area smooth; beads were also drilled this way, some of them being quite delicate. Segments of circles were made by holding a tubular drill at a slant, and straight lines were often done by scratching with a flint knife.

Northwest Indians discovered early that the hollow reed drill worked best and that sand abrasive embedded itself in a softer reed and lengthened its useful life. Harder drills wore out faster because the sand grains could not embed themselves.

Little archeological evidence remains of carving methods used by ancient Chinese and Central American jade lapidaries, but the carvings themselves give some indication of the process. Since the Chinese developed carving techniques that enabled them quickly to advance to productions beyond anything attempted by the Maori, they must have invented a larger variety of working tools. In addition, better lubricants than water and harder abrasives than sand must have been discovered.

This brings up the recurring question of whether or not early Chinese carvers were familiar with diamond as an abrasive. Analysis of Chinese texts establishes that trade involving engraving tools took place through intermediaries between Rome and China, beginning at about 168 B.C. No clear evidence

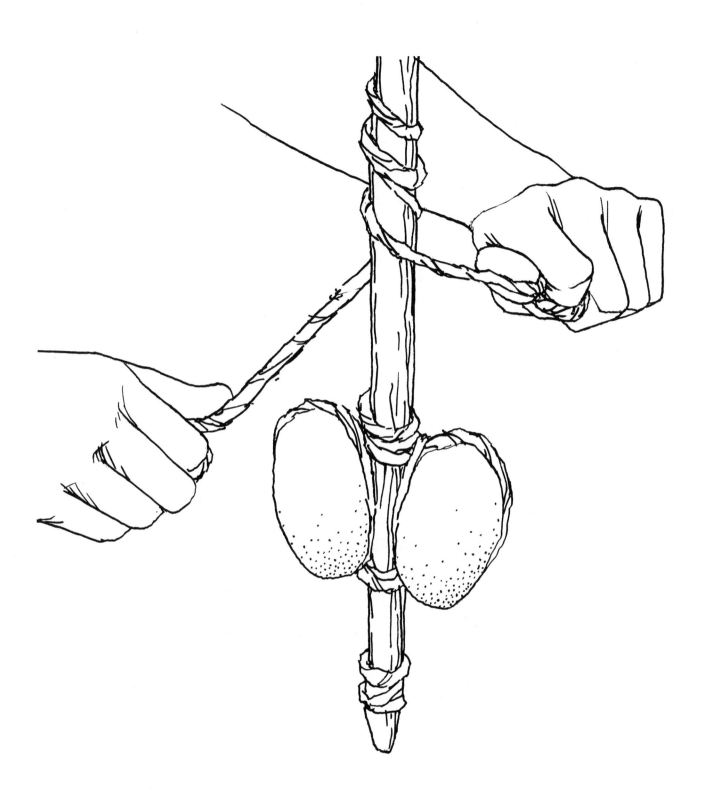

One type of Maori jade drill with balanced stone flyweights.

exists, however, that these tools were diamond-tipped. The date of first diamond use in China remains obscure, but from the third century A.D. onward, Chinese familiarity with diamond is attested, and records even include acknowledgment of India as the source of this familiarity. India had been exporting diamonds as early as the fourth century B.C., so a very strong possibility exists that at least some Chinese carvers were using diamond for carving before the birth of Christ, even though direct evidence is not yet available.

Speculation has been raised that the Chinese did not develop a drill until several centuries after they began to cut jade. Time has erased most of the evidence, but—considering the rapid improvement in carving—the drill could not have been too late in appearing. Rather than boring simple holes, the Chinese developed some clever techniques using the hollow reed drill and later the hollow cast-bronze tube drill, both of which were rotated rapidly and fed with abrasives to cut cores in stone.

Several sizes of core drills were used, from large-diameter cylinders to the very small central core drill. With a sharp blow of a hammer, a small core could be broken loose, leaving a smooth-sided hole. Around this hole a larger core could be drilled and then removed by undercutting it from the base of the smaller core hole. This method required removal of far less material than would be required by simple abrasion. Furthermore, use of cylindrical core

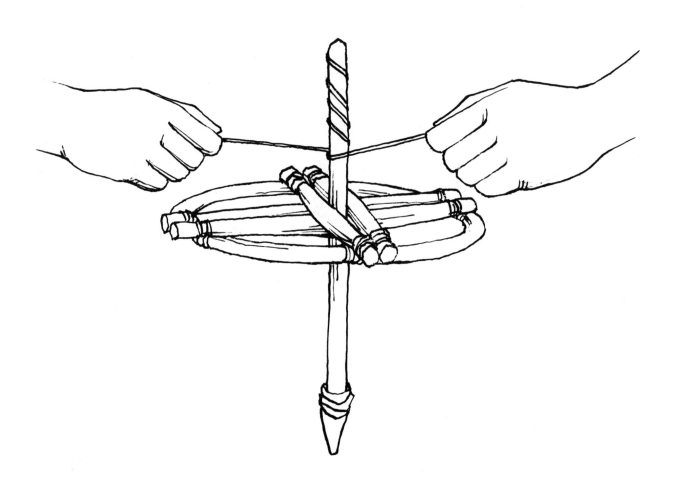

Another type of Maori jade drill with bent-twig flywheel.

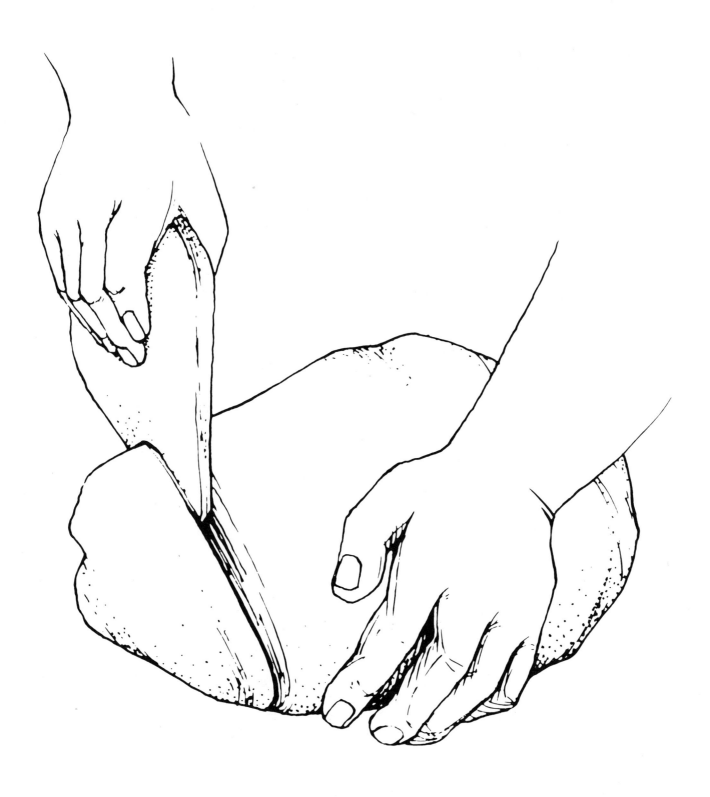

Sandstone slab method used by Northwest Indians for sawing jade.

drills enabled artisans to create very large and deep holes.

Some drills were operated by rapid rotation between the palms as ground abrasive and lubricant were fed to the working surface. This seems to have been the method favored by Central American lapidaries, as well. The Chinese later also developed mechanized drills, whose hollow rods were driven by modified forms of the same cord-and-bow arrangement used by American Indians for fire-making drills.

From the beginning, all jade culture artisans performed some sort of sawing or slabbing operation. For example, the earliest Chinese jades were commonly carved from slabs ½ inch or less in thickness. Present gaps in our knowledge make it difficult to say whether the slabbing of jade was due to a shortage of material or to difficulties in forming thicker objects. Perhaps it was just a matter of custom.

Artifacts recovered in the Fraser River area of British Columbia show conclusively that the natives there successfully used thin, flat slabs of bedded sandstone to saw through jade. The process must have been slow and wasteful of jade, but it was effective. First the jade piece was sawed partway through on one side; then it was turned over and sawed partway through on the other side. The bridge between the two cuts was then broken by a

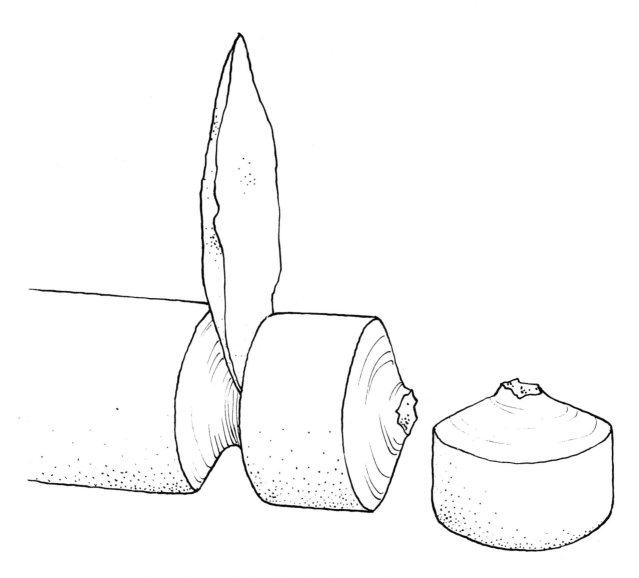

Primitive Maori method for sawing nephrite by rubbing it with an edged stone.

Traditional Chinese method for sawing a jade boulder with a two-man saw. In this fanciful scene, the process looks clean, effortless, and leisurely, which it certainly was not.

sharp blow, saving untold hours of further sawing. The exposed ragged edges could then be rubbed off to smooth the slab. The Maori, Mesoamericans, and Chinese used similar methods.

The subsequent introduction of the vegetable-fiber cord saw constituted a definite technological improvement. Such a cord, drawn back and forth as abrasive and water are fed to it, cuts hard stone surprisingly quickly. Even today the old method persists, with several strands of twisted wire taking the place of cord, the wire being strung on a bowlike wooden frame to provide tension and make it easier to use.

Although no one knows the details of the earliest techniques and tools, rubbing sticks of various designs, sand abrasive, and quantities of time and patience were essentially all the ancients used. Hand-held grinding stones were worked over the carving, with water added; or the grinding stone was rested on the ground or placed under water, and the carving was stroked back and forth upon it.

Introduction of the rotary drill made it possible to add in-the-round structure and detail to the carvings and to make hollow objects such as vases and snuff bottles. These were (and are) always hollowed out before work commenced on the outside surface of the carving. In the course of development, drills were fitted with points of obsidian, flint, quartz, and so on of various sizes and shapes.

Still later, a cord stretched over a bow was wrapped around the shaft, which was then turned by stroking the bow back and forth—the first mechanization of the drill operation. The use of bow drills is evident in many ancient cultures and is even illustrated on an ancient Egyptian monument. From the bow drill to a kind of horizontal spindle

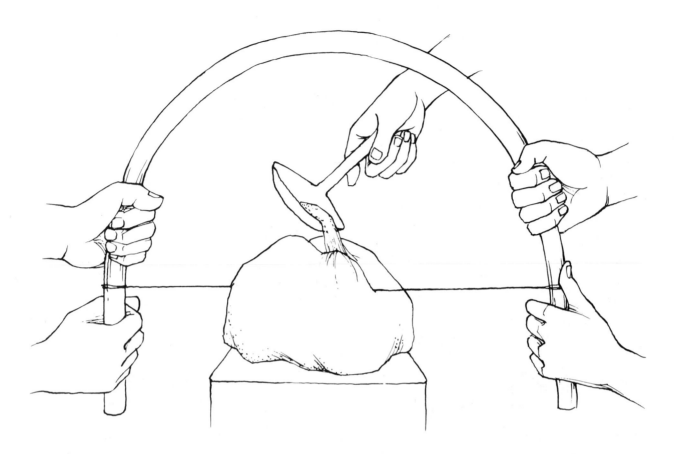

Diagram of the Chinese two-man jade saw, or ssu tzu. *The helper adds cutting abrasive.*

lathe, also driven by a cord or belt arrangement, was only a short step. This and the foot-treadle attachment to move the cord or belt were the only fundamental mechanical improvements in this device in thousands of years. Since metal was introduced into Chinese technology centuries after jade carving had been mastered, it had almost no effect on the basic carving methods; it did, however, allow manufacture of tools for sawing, drilling, and grinding, which in turn contributed to producing the far more complicated carvings of later centuries.

Abrasives and Polishing Powders

Like the whole technology of jade carving in China, development of abrasives advanced slowly. The earliest abrasive was probably crushed quartz or quartz sand, which is almost always readily available and continues to be widely used for many abrasive pur-

poses today. Its relatively low durability rendered work slower and more tedious and generally limited carving to flat and thin pieces inscribed with low-relief surface decoration.

A switch from sand to crushed garnet, with its combination of superior hardness and sharp-angled grains, occurred centuries before the beginning of the Christian era. The chief gain was in time saved; control of the shape and finish for each carved piece was reduced because of the greater cutting speed. Diamond tools—though known by this time—were too rare and costly to be in general use. Metal tools, which had been introduced by the end of the Chou Dynasty, were combined at about 500 B.C. with the newer garnet abrasive to ensure that almost any form could be executed in jade. As nothing more was needed to produce finished forms of all kinds, a great delay ensued before any significant change came to the native cutting industry.

After another fifteen or sixteen centuries, the next improvement in abrasives—from garnet to corundum—came about; as before, time-saving was the major gain. The final revolution in abrasives

Maori method for shaping a nephrite adze by rubbing it on a water-lubricated sandstone slab.

came at the very end of the 1800s when man-made silicon carbide, with its superior cutting qualities and low cost, was introduced into China.

The incredibly slow changes in tools and abrasives over forty centuries have finally made it possible to produce a very intricate jade piece in a relatively short time. Many jade connoisseurs, however, argue that the older carvings, made before all the changes, were better. Labor costs and the ultimate cost of the final carving were of little concern in the Ching Dynasty's emperor-supported shops, nor are they now for high-quality carvings privately commissioned through modern shops. Like most older carvings, these are hand-rubbed, meticulously cut, and seem to have smoother surfaces and fewer visible cutting errors (such as rough edges and irregular fine lines).

Work on old carvings was so laborious and proceeded so slowly that the artisan had plenty of time to think about the product and ran very little risk of making a faulty cut that might require alteration of the original carving plan. One glance at the merchandise in a present-day Hong Kong jade shop illustrates the decline in the high art of jade carving fostered by rapid mass production with diamond abrasives and power machinery. Labor and other overhead costs are an important factor in the operation of these shops, so short-cut carving—which tends to produce objects with too many flat-slabbed surfaces and too high a polish—becomes the norm.

By now almost every hard material imaginable has been pressed into service and tried as a jade abrasive. Crushed sand, garnet, and corundum have proved their worth and are still used in some locales. For centuries, the favorites for jade carving had always been crushed corundum or emery, a granular material consisting of corundum mixed with magnetite or hematite. When man-made silicon carbide was finally introduced as an abrasive, its impact was revolutionary.

Silicon carbide—known commercially by names such as Carborundum and Crystolon—is harder (9½) than natural corundum (9). For abrasive purposes, the material is crushed and then accurately separated and graded by the size of the grit particles. A typical modern coarse grit, called 100 mesh, has particles that average about $1/170$ inch in diameter. Such grit is ordinarily used for rough grinding, either as a loose powder or bonded to a grinding wheel. The name *100 mesh* refers to the fact that particles of this size will pass through a screen that has 100 equal-sized mesh holes to the inch. In a grit of 220 mesh, the particle size averages half that of 100, and so on to such small sizes as 1200 mesh, which is used for the last fine grinding stage before polishing.

Powders for polishing must contain extremely small particles to avoid scratching an already fine-ground surface. Some polishing powders have been known since antiquity, the best of these being rouge, a powdered iron oxide. The process of polishing differs from that of grinding in significant ways. While being rubbed rapidly with a polishing powder, a carved jade surface may do one of two things. First, the surface may actually become hot enough for local melting to occur, creating a very thin layer of melted glaze and giving the surface a high reflective luster. Second, even if the melting point of the material is too high for local fusion, or if such fusion does not occur for some other reason, the abrasion of the polishing powder may smooth out the tiny scratches left from the last grinding.

The polishing powder does not have to be harder than the material it is polishing, as long as it can develop enough localized frictional heat. Some old-time artisans insist that one of the best polishing powders is crushed jade itself. Nevertheless, if cost is not a deterrent, diamond—the hardest substance known—is almost universally considered the best grinding and polishing agent available. For heavy sawing of smaller pieces, diamond of 50 to 100 mesh is used; coarse grinding mesh if 400 to 600; and fine grinding mesh is 800 to 1200. Diamond polishing powders are prepared in mesh sizes from 3200 to 6400.

Modern cutters still find nephrite and jadeite difficult to polish and most prefer chromic oxide as a polishing powder because it is inexpensive and green-colored (rendering it less obvious if it becomes lodged in tiny cracks during polishing). If cost is a deterrent, cerium oxide, aluminum oxide, and tin oxide can be used and are available in pure form for the lapidary. The most satisfactory polishing powders other than diamond, however, are synthetically prepared materials such as Linde A. Regardless of what grinding and polishing powders are used, jadeite must be processed with hard surface laps through all stages to avoid severe undercutting.

Modern Cutting and Carving Operations

The saw is basic to all jade lapidary operations. Perhaps the modern saw should be called a disk scratcher or band scratcher, since the word *saw* tends to evoke images of teeth—which the lapidary saw does not have. A person can press a finger lightly against the edge of a lapidary saw blade while it is in motion and not be cut because the tiny abrasive particles of its cutting edge are too fine to cut the skin.

A typical modern lapidary saw is made of a thin disk of bronze or cold-rolled steel set on an axle that can be turned at different speeds by an electric motor with pulley arrangements. There are two types of disks: one has notches cut across its rim and diamond grit hammered into them; the other has diamond powder fixed firmly to the rim by sintering, or heating, with powdered metal. This powder-metallurgy process permits metallic bonding of the diamond grit at temperatures low enough that the diamond is not destroyed.

Saw blades, of course, are manufactured in various diameters and thicknesses for different purposes. Slabbing saws are larger (sometimes quite large), with coarser grit. Ingeniously rigged slabbing saws as large as 3 feet in diameter have been used in remote Alaskan and Canadian jade fields—powered by local watercourses or gasoline engines—to reduce large boulders to transportable size. In the New Zealand mountains, two-man steel saws impregnated with diamond have been used for the same purpose.

Trim saws use smaller, thinner, lighter blades and operate at higher speeds. For slitting very valuable jades, paper-thin blades that rotate at high speeds are available. All saw blades are lubricated to keep them cool during cutting so that they do not warp or overheat the material being cut. In the early days of this century, an excellent lubricant for saws could be concocted at home from kerosene and motor oil. Later, oil companies developed more satisfactory and less hazardous lubricants.

Jade for jewelry is most frequently cut into what is called cabochon form. The word *cabochon* is derived from the old French word *caboche*, meaning "head" and referring to the rounded or domed tops of the finished stone. Most jade cabochons are oval in outline and flat on one side, but variations on the theme are common.

Chinese jade cutter, in the 1920s, using foot-treadle-powered circular saw blade to reduce rough jade to smaller pieces.

The cabochon starts on the saw. With any jade saw, the material to be cut is pressed firmly against the edge of the moving blade, either by hand or (better) with a mechanical feeding device, until the diamond-edged blade literally scratches its way through. Because of its extreme hardness, the blade cuts quite rapidly. The jade rough is next sliced into appropriately sized and carefully selected pieces, using as many saw cuts as necessary. Each selected piece must now be ground to a shape approximating its final form. The method of doing this varies, depending on the final form to be achieved and the value of the material.

In ordinary work, to strip off the first rough projections and unwanted material, grinders are used. These are rotating wheels, commonly made of silicon carbide, which has been strongly bonded together by being mixed with clay and various bonding agents and then heated to a high temperature. The wheels are made in various sizes, such as 6-, 8-, and 10-inch diameters; the wheels' thickness increases with their diameter, from 1 to 1½ inches, to maintain physical strength at high rotation rates. Grinding wheels are usually made of either 100 or 220 grit abrasive and are kept water-cooled when in use.

Whatever kind of grinding wheel is used, holding the slippery cabochon in hand during the operation, as is still done in more primitive cutting shops, provides an unsteady base (as well as being unsafe). To eliminate most of the danger, and to make it easier to see the work in progress, the cabochon is usually mounted on a dop stick—a short piece of wooden dowel selected to fit the size of the cabochon. A dop stick may even be as thick as a broom stick, if needed. The rough-ground cabochon is heated and then fastened to the end of the dop stick with a special heated and softened dopping wax, which is molded beneath to support the cabochon during the remaining cutting operations.

Once grinding is completed and the cabochon is properly shaped, with all large scratches and blemishes worked out, the piece is ready for sanding. The purpose of sanding is to remove the grinding scratches (or rather to replace them with finer scratches) while perfecting the shape. Sanding can be done wet or dry; in either case—except for the presence or absence of cooling water—the equipment and its operation are about the same. Sanding grits are most common in 100 and 220 mesh, but they are available up to 600 mesh. The abrasive is bonded to the face of a flat disk, which fastens easily to the face of a rotating plate; this plate is sometimes attached to the same axle that holds the grinding wheel. Alternatively, the abrasive may be bonded to a continuous belt that fits an expanding drum rotating on the same axle. Most lapidary equipment is designed to allow rapid changing of sanding cloth disks or belts.

Now the moment for polishing arrives, the moment that will tell whether the preliminary grinding and sanding work was properly done. All sorts of polishing devices are available, but rotating buffs of leather or felt are generally preferred. Water is applied to keep the buff damp and to help hold the abrasive polishing paste, which is smeared on as needed. Light pressure and slight movement of the stone (still held on the dop stick) over the buff continues; then suddenly the lapidary no longer holds a common stone on the end of a stick, but an object of beauty—a gem.

Carving jade, like cutting cabochons, is a matter of removing unwanted material by sawing and grinding. To accomplish this, the carver must have a strong mental image of the finished work throughout the process.

In addition to various pieces of lapidary equipment already mentioned, some special carving tools are required, including a machine called a point carver. This is a motor-driven, rapidly rotating spindle, on one end of which is a chuck for holding soft iron tools of various shapes. Grit and lubricant are fed to the stone as it is worked against the rotating tool point. Of course, carbide- or diamond-tipped tools can also be used, at greater expense.

Hole cutters, internal grinders, special machine rigs with flexible drive shafts, and many others compose the arsenal of special devices. Simple forms such as vases and goblets—including the beautiful, highly polished nephrite objects coming from Russia in recent years—are cut on lapidary lathes that use various kinds of lapidary grinders and polishers rather than the steel cutting blades that are more commonly used in lathe work.

In spite of the flood of mass-produced carvings for the tourist trade, very fine jade pieces are still being prepared in Asia, Europe, New Zealand, and elsewhere. An increasing number of hobbyists and artists have turned to stone carving (particularly of jade), as equipment technology has steadily improved. Most carvers prefer to work on small pieces, but the upper size limit is set only by the weight they can handle—alone or with the help of hoisting machinery. Stone carvings many feet tall are not uncommon. Of course, with jade, the value and size of available pieces of rough material usually impose strict limits on the size of carvings.

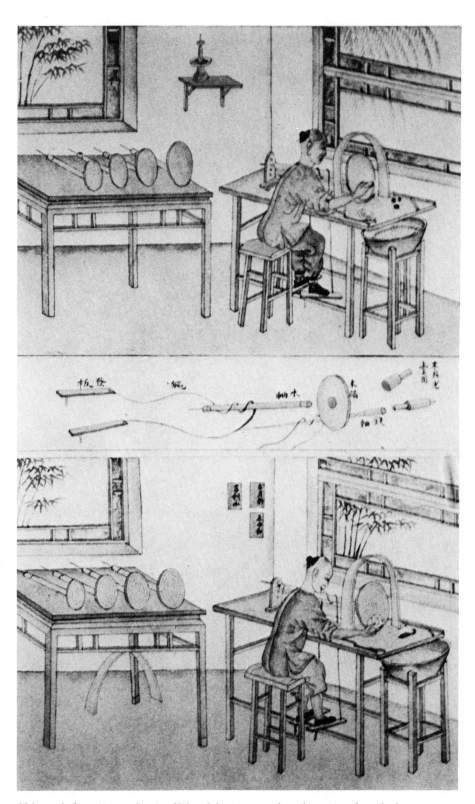

Chinese jade cutters using traditional foot-powered equipment and methods.

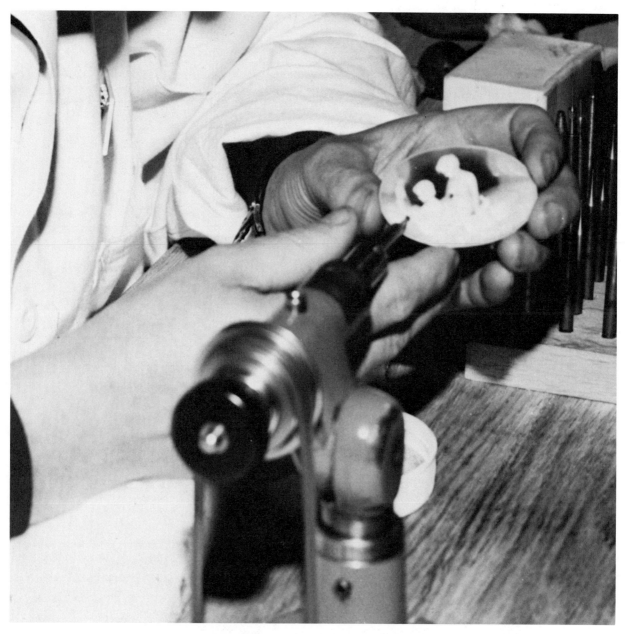

Highly skilled artisan using a motor-driven point carver for detailed finishing work. In a modern, well-equipped carving shop such as this one, a wide array of efficient working tools is available for every need.

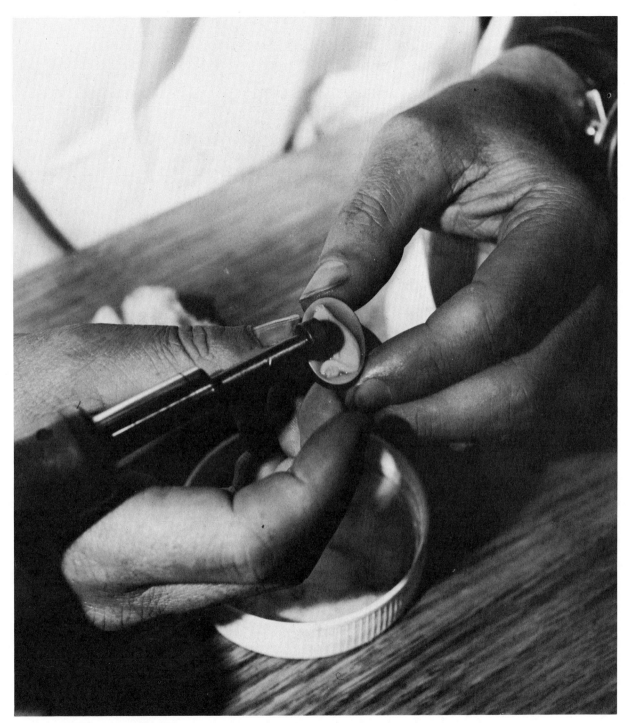

For present-day carvers of jade, motor-driven grinders, polishers, carvers, and other tools can be fastened interchangeably to a motor-driven shaft or, if desired, to the end of a flexible shaft. In this case, the piece is moved by hand to contact the rotating tool. When a flexible shaft is used, the piece can remain stationary while the tool is moved over it.

Chinese jade carver, in the 1920s, using foot-treadle power to turn a small metal carving wheel to cut his design. The same technique is still used in some parts of China today.

Foot-treadle power turns a small polishing wheel for this carver in the 1920s. Time-consuming care at this stage could determine the quality of the carving's appearance. Machinery in China today may be improved but the carving process remains the same.

BIBLIOGRAPHY

Abel-Vidor, S., et al. 1981. *Between continents/between seas: Precolumbian art of Costa Rica.* New York: Harry Abrams.

Ashley, R. 1973. Jade man down under. *Arts of Asia* 3(2).

Balser, C. 1968. Metal and jade in lower Central America. In *Actas y memorias del XXXVII Congresso Internacional de Americanistas, Republica Argentina, 1966.* Vol. 4, pp. 57–66. Buenos Aires: Congresso Internacional de Americanistas.

———. 1974. *El jade de Costa Rica.* San Jose, Costa Rica: Libreria Lehmann.

Bergsten, L. J. 1964. Inclusions in jade. *Lapidary Journal* 17: 1076, 1196.

Bishop, H. R. 1906. *Investigations and studies in jade.* 2 vols. Privately printed. New York.

Born, G. M. 1982. *Chinese jade: An annotated bibliography.* Chicago: Celadon Press.

Bradt, R. C. et al. 1973. The toughness of jade. *American Mineralogist* 58: 727–32.

Branham, A. W. 1941. Jade in Wyoming. *The Mineralogist* (March 1941).

———. 1944. Jade—Wyoming and Oriental. *The Mineralogist* (January 1944).

———. 1946. A new discovery of jade that resembles Fraser River material. *Rocks and Minerals* (December 1946).

———. 1947. The finding of a great gem stone. *Rocks and Minerals* (May 1947).

———. 1950. Jade is where you find it. *The Mineralogist* (May 1950).

Burwell, W. B. 1948. Exhibition of Chinese jades—OAC London. *Oriental Art* (Autumn 1948).

Bushnell, G. H. S. 1965. *Ancient arts of the Americas.* New York: Frederick A. Praeger.

Carochi, H. 1645. *Compedio de arte de la lengua Mexicana.* ed. J. Gonzales and Juan de Montoya. Puebla, Mexico. 1910.

Caso, A. 1965. Lapidary work, gold work, and copper work from Oaxaca. In *Handbook of Middle American Indians,* vol. 3. Austin: University of Texas Press.

Cheng, T. 1969. *Jade flowers and floral patterns in Chinese decorative art.* Hong Kong: Carlson Printers.

Chibber, H. L. 1934. *The mineral resources of Burma.* London: Macmillan.

Chihara, K. 1971. Mineralogy and paragenesis of jadeites from the Omi-Kotaki area, Central Japan. Mineral Society of Japan, Special Paper 1.

Chu, A., and Chu, G. 1978. *The collector's book of jade.* New York: Crown Publishers.

Clarke, F. W., and Merrill, G. P. 1888. On nephrite and jadeite. *Proceedings of the U.S. National Museum* 11: 115–30.

Cobb, H. 1949. The Long Creek jade deposit. *The Mineralogist* (January 1949).

Coleman, R. 1980. The natural occurrence of jade

and its bearing on the sources of Mesoamerican jade artifacts. Paper delivered at Mesoamerican–Central American Jade Conference, Dumbarton Oaks, Washington, D.C.

Cortez, H. 1519. Merced de Hernan Cortez á los caciques de Axapusco. In Joaquin Garcia Icazbalcita, ed., *Coleccion de documentos para la historia de Mexico*, 2 (7–8), 1866.

Couper, Hey, and Hutchinson. 1981. Cosmochlor— a new examination. *Mineralogical Magazine* 4.

Covarrubias, M. 1957. *Indian art of Mexico and Central America*. New York: Alfred A. Knopf.

Crippen, R. A., Jr. 1951. *Nephrite jade and associated rocks of the Cape San Martin region, Monterey County, California*. California Division of Mines, Special Report 10A.

Dake, H. C. 1942. Jade in Wyoming, new discoveries. *The Mineralogist* (September 1942).

———. 1948. Jade—oldest gem stone known. *The Mineralogist* (January 1948).

Damour, A. 1846. Analyses du jade oriental. *Annals of Chemistry and Physics*, 3d series, 16: 469–74.

———. 1863. Notice et analyse sur le jade verte: Réunion de cettes matiere mineral a la famille wernerites. *Comptes Rendus* 56: 861–65.

———. 1865. Sur la composition des haches en pierre trouvées dans les monuments Celtiques et chez les tribes sauvages. *Comptes Rendus* 61: 357–68.

———. 1881. Nouvelles analyses sur la jadeite et sur quelques roches sodiferes. *Bulletin Société Minéralogique de France*. 4: 156–60.

d'Argence, R-Y.L. 1972. *Chinese jades in the Avery Brundage collection*. Japan: Kodansha International.

De Roever, W. F. 1955. Genesis of jadeite by low grade metamorphism. *American Journal of Science* 253: 283–98.

Desautels, P. E. 1968. *The mineral kingdom*. New York: Grosset & Dunlap.

———. 1971. *The gem kingdom*. New York: Random House.

Diaz de Castillo, B. 1632. *Historia verdadera de la conquista de la Nueva España*. Trans. A. P. Maudslay. London: Hakluyt Society, 1901.

Digby, A. 1964. *Maya jades*. London: British Museum.

Dobretsov, N. L. 1968. Miscibility limits and mean composition of jadeite pyroxenes. Doklady Akademie Nauk Series, Vol. 146.

Drucker, P. 1955. The Cerro de las Mesas offering of jade and other materials. Bureau of American Ethnology Bulletin 157, Anthropological Papers 44. Washington: Smithsonian Institution.

Durán, Friar D. 1581. *The Aztecs: The history of the Indies of New Spain*. Doris Heyden and Fernando Horcasitas, trans. New York: Orion Press. 1964.

Easby, E. K. 1961. The Squier jades from Tonina, Chiapas. In S. K. Lothrop et al., *Essays in pre-Columbian art and archeology*. Cambridge, Massachusetts: Harvard University Press.

———. 1968. *Pre-Columbian jade from Costa Rica*. New York: Andre Emmerich.

Emmons, G. T. 1923. *Jade in British Columbia and Alaska and its use by the natives*. Indian Notes and Monograph Series #35, Museum of the American Indian. New York: Heye Foundation.

Fischer, H. 1880. *Nephrit und Jadeite nach ihren mineralogischen Eigenschaften sowie nach ihrer urgeschichtlichen und ethnographischen Bedeutung*, 2d ed. Stuttgart.

Foshag, W. F. 1938. *Minerals from earth and sky*. Vol. 3. Smithsonian Scientific Series. Washington: Smithsonian Institution.

———. 1957. *Mineralogical studies in Guatemalan jade*. U.S. National Museum Publication 4307. Washington: U.S. National Museum.

Foshag, W. F., and Leslie, R. 1955. Jadeite from Manzanal, Guatemala. *American Antiquity* 21: 81–83.

Gardner, M. 1974. The combinatorial basis of the *I Ching*, the Chinese book of divination and wisdom. *Scientific American* (Jan.): 109.

Garber, J. 1980. Patterns of jade consumption and disposal at the late pre-classic center of Cerros, Northern Belize. Paper presented at the Mesoamerican–Central American Jade Conference, Dumbarton Oaks, Washington, D.C.

Gems and Gemology. 1982. Vol. 18 (jade issue) (Spring 1982).

Gems and Minerals. 1961. The art of feeling jade. *Gems and Minerals* 286: 28–29.

Goette, J. 1937. *Jade lore*. New York: Reynal & Hitchcock.

Gomara, F. L. de. 1552. *La conquista de Mexico*. Zaragosa, Spain. 1943.

Gosse, R. C. 1962. Jade of Wyoming. *Rocks and Minerals* (May–June 1962).

Gump, A. L. 1937. *Jade hunt*. San Francisco: H. S. Crocker.

Gump, R. 1962. *Jade: Stone of heaven*. Garden City, New York: Doubleday & Co.

Hammond, N. A., et al. 1977. Maya jade: Source location and analysis. In T. K. Earle and J. E. Ericson, eds., *Exchange analysis systems in prehistory*, pp. 35–67. New York: Academic Press.

Hansford, S. H. 1948. Chinese jade. *Transactions of the Oriental Ceramic Society*. London: Oriental Ceramic Society.

———. 1950. *Chinese jade carving*. London: Lund Humphries & Co.

———. 1968. *Chinese carved jades*. Greenwich, Connecticut: New York Graphic Society.

———. 1970. *Jade: Essence of hills and streams*. London: University of London.

Hardinge, Sir C. 1961. *Jade fact and fable*. London: Luzac & Co.

———. 1953. Jade: A problem in nomenclature. *Journal of Gemmology* 14 (3): 112–17.

Hartman, J. M. 1969. *Chinese jade of five centuries*. Rutland, Vermont: Charles E. Tuttle.

———. 1974. The Bishop Jade Collection. *Arts of Asia* (3).

Hemrich, G. 1966. *Jade*. California: Gembooks.

Iwao, S. 1953. *Albitite and associated jadeite rock from Kataki District Japan: A study in ceramic raw material*. Report of the Geological Survey of Japan #153.

Jenyns, S. 1951. *Chinese archaic jades*. London: British Museum.

Jobbins, E. A., and Rutland, E. H. 1974. Sausserite as a jade simulant. *Journal of Gemmology* 14 (1): 1–7.

Kane, M. 1965. Rock hunting in Wyoming. *Rocks and Minerals* (August 1965).

Keverne, R. 1975. Jade: A review of the exhibition at the Victoria and Albert Museum, London. *Arts of Asia* 5(4).

Kraft, J. L. 1947. *Adventures in jade*. New York: Henry Holt.

Kunz, G. F. 1913. *The curious lore of precious stones*. Reprint. New York: Dover Publications, 1971.

———. 1913. *Gems and precious stones of North America*. Reprint. New York: Dover Publications, 1968.

Lacroix, A. 1930. La jadeite de Bermanie: Les roches qu'elle constitue ou qui l'accompagnent: Composition et origine. *Bulletin Société Minéralogique France* 53.

Lanning, John Tate. 1939. Lo que enbió de la Nueva España el Capitán Hernando Cortez. *Review History America* 1.

Lapidary Journal. [Many articles on jade, spanning several decades.]

Laufer, B. 1912. *Jade: A study in Chinese archeology and religion*. Reprint. New York: Dover Publications, 1974.

Leary, R. H. 1973. Jade mining in Canada. *Arts of Asia* 3(5).

Li-ping, T., et al. 1978. *A mineralogical study of the Fengtien nephrite deposits of Hualien*. Taipei: Taiwan National Science Council.

Lothrop, S. K. 1955. Jade and string sawings in northeastern Costa Rica. *American Antiquity* 21: 43–51.

Luzzatti-Bilitz, O. 1969. *Antique jade*. London: Hamlyn House.

Madson, M. E. 1975. *The Wyoming jade story*. Riverton, Wyoming: M. E. Madson.

Mallory, L. D. 1971. Jadeite in Middle America. *Lapidary Journal* (December 1971): 1196.

Martin, R. I. 1946. Jade is where you find it. *The Mineralogist* (February 1946).

McBirney, A. R., et al. 1967. Eclogites and jadeites from the Motagua fault zone, Guatemala. *American Mineralogist* 53: 908–18.

Mena, R. 1927. *Catalogue de la coleccion de objetos de jade*. Mexico City: Museo Nacional, Departimiento de Arqueologia.

Monardes, N. 1569. *Historia medicinal de las cosas que se traen de las Indias Occidentales que sirven en medicina*. Ed. Sir Stephen Gaselee. London. 1925.

Museo Nacional de Costa Rica. *The aboriginal jade of Costa Rica*. San Jose, Costa Rica: Museo Nacional.

National Museum of History of Taipei, Taiwan, Republic of China. 1984. *Chinese jade* [exhibition at the Fresno Metropolitan Museum of Art, History, and Science, April, 1984].

———. 1967. *Illustrated handbook, Chinese cultural art treasures*. Taipei: National Museum of History.

National Palace Museum. 1969. *Masterworks of Chinese jade in the National Museum*. Taipei: National Palace Museum.

Ng, J. Y., and Root, E. 1984. *Jade for you*. Los Angeles: Jade and Gem Corporation of America.

Norman, D., and Johnson, W. A. 1941. Note on spectographic study of Central American and Asiatic jades. *Journal of the Optical Society of America* 31.

Nott, S. C. 1942. *Chinese jades in the Stanley*

Charles Nott Collection. West Palm Beach, Florida: Norton Gallery and School of Art.

————. 1947. *Voices from the flowery kingdom*. Brattleboro, Vermont: F. L. Hildreth & Co.

————. 1962. *Chinese jade throughout the ages*. Rutland, Vermont: Charles E. Tuttle.

Palmer, J. P. 1967. *Jade*. London: Spring Art Books.

Peterson, K. 1962. *Ancient Mexico*. New York: Capricorn Books.

Pope-Hennessey, U. 1923. *Early Chinese jades*. New York: Frederick A. Stokes.

————. 1946. *A jade miscellany*. London: Nicholson and Watson.

Proskouriakoff, T. 1974. Jades from the cenote of sacrifice, Chichen Itza, Yucatan. *Memoirs of the Peabody Museum of Archeology and Ethnology, Harvard* 10(1).

Read, A. W. 1950. *An illustrated encyclopedia of Maori life*. Wellington, New Zealand: Read.

Rhoads, B. 1943. Hunting jade in Wyoming. *The Mineralogist* (December 1943).

Ruff, E. 1950. *Jade of the Maori*. London: Gemmological Association of Great Britain.

Sahagun, Friar B. de. 1558–59. *General history of the things of New Spain*. Florentine Codex, Book II. Trans. Arthur Anderson and Charles Dibble. Santa Fe: School of American Research, University of Utah, 1955.

Sakikawa, N. 1968. *Jade*. Tokyo: Japan Publications.

Salmony, A. 1941. *A catalogue of jade*. New York: Vassar College Art Gallery.

————. 1963. *Chinese jade through the Wei Dynasty*. New York: Ronald Press.

Savage, G. 1965. *Chinese jade: A concise introduction*. New York: October House.

Schoon, T. 1973. *Jade country*. Sydney, Australia: Jade Arts.

Shedel, J. J. 1974. *The splendor of jade*. New York: E. P. Dutton & Co.

Sherer, R. L. 1969. Nephrite deposits of the Granite, the Seminoe, and the Laramie mountains, Wyoming. Thesis, University of Wyoming (Laramie, Wyoming).

Shook, E. M. 1945. Archeological discovery at Finca Arizona, Guatemala. *Notes on Middle American Archeology and Ethnology* 2(57): 200–221. Carnegie Institution of Washington, Division of Historical Research, Cambridge, Massachusetts.

Shook, E. M., and Kidder A. V. 1952. Mound E-111-3, Kaminaljuyu, Guatemala. *Contributions to American Anthropology and History* 2(53): 33–123. Carnegie Institution of Washington, Pub. 596.

Silva, Z. C. 1967. Studies on jadeites and albitites from Guatemala. Master's thesis, Rice University (Houston, Texas).

Sinkankas, J. 1959, 1976. *Gemstones of North America*. 2 vols. New York: Van Nostrand Reinhold.

————. 1968. *Van Nostrand's standard catalog of gems*. New York: Van Nostrand Reinhold.

Smith, A. L., and Kidder, A. V. 1943. Explorations in the Motagua Valley, Guatemala. *Contributions to American Anthropology and History* 8(41): 101–82. Carnegie Institution of Washington, Pub. 546.

Sterling, M. W. 1968. Aboriginal jade use in the New World. In *Actas y memorias del XXXVII Congreso Internacional de Americanistas, Republica Argentina*, 1966. Vol. 4. Buenos Aires: Congreso Internacional de Americanistas.

Tan, L. P., et al. *Mineralogy of the nephrite in the Fengtien area, Haulien, Taiwan*. Taipei: National Science Council.

Turner, F. J. 1936. Geological investigation of the nephrites, serpentines, and related "greenstones" used by the Maoris of Otago and South Canterbury. *Transactions of the Royal Society* 15: 187–210.

Vaillant, G. C. 1930. Excavations at Zacatenco. *American Museum of Natural History, Anthropological Papers* 32(1).

————. 1934. Excavations at Gualupita. *American Museum of Natural History, Anthropological Papers* 35(1).

————. 1935. Excavations at El Arbolillo. *American Museum of Natural History, Anthropological Papers* 35(2).

Washington, H. S. 1922. The jade of the Tuxtla statuette. *Proceedings of the U.S. National Museum* 60(14).

————. 1922. The jades of Middle America. *Proceedings of the National Academy of Sciences* 8(11): 319–26.

Watson, W. 1963. *Chinese jades in the Chester Beatty Library*. Dublin: Hodges and Figgis.

————. 1973. *The genius of China*. Catalog of the Royal Academy exhibition of Chinese archeological finds, Sept. 1973 to Jan. 1974. London: Times Newspapers Ltd.

Webster, R. 1953. Jade and jadelike minerals. *The Mineralogist* (December 1953).

Williams, C. A. S. 1960. *Encyclopedia of Chinese symbolism and art motives.* New York: Julian Press.

Wills, G. 1964. *Jade.* London: Arco.

————. 1972. *Jade: A collector's guide.* South Brunswick, New Jersey: A. S. Barnes & Co.

————. 1981. *Jade of the East.* New York: John Weatherkill.

Wobber, D. *Jade beneath the sea—a diving adventure.* Pacific Grove, California: Boxwood Press.

Yoder, H. S., Jr. 1950. The jadeite problem. *American Journal of Science* 248(4, 5): 225–48, 312–34.

Yoder, H. S., Jr., and Chesterman, C. W. 1951. *Jadeite in San Benito County, California.* California Division of Mines, Special Report 10-C.

Yueh, C. 1975. Nephrite deposits and mining industries of Taiwan. Taiwan Bureau of Mines Survey Report, September 1975.

Zara, L. 1969. *Jade.* New York: Walker & Co.

Zhi-ren, Q. 1971. Jade in ancient china. *Arts of Asia* 1(1).

Zodac, P. 1939. Nephrite and jadeite in Washington. *Rocks and Minerals* (April 1939).

————. 1939. Nephrite in Wyoming. *Rocks and Minerals* (July 1939).

INDEX